Betty McLellan is a feminist psychotherapist with more than twenty years experience. She works with women and men in individual and couple counselling and facilitates groups for women and men separately and then together. The best relationships, she believes, are those where there is mutual respect, honesty and love. She is the author of *Overcoming Anxiety* (1992) and *Beyond Psychoppression* (1995). She lives in Townsville, Queensland.

Other books by the same author

Overcoming Anxiety
Beyond Psychoppression

Help! I'm Living with a ~~Man~~ *Boy* has been translated into numerous languages. To see a complete list of these, please visit our website: www.spinifexpress.com.au

BETTY McLELLAN
HELP!
I'M LIVING
WITH
A ~~MAN~~ *Boy*

*S*PINIFEX

Spinifex Press Pty Ltd
504 Queensberry Street
North Melbourne, Vic. 3051
Australia
women@spinifexpress.com.au
http://www.spinifexpress.com.au

First published by Spinifex Press, 1999
Second edition 2006

Copying for educational purposes

Edited by Janet Mackenzie
Typeset in Sabon by Palmer Higgs Pty Ltd
Cover design by Deb Snibson

Printed and bound by McPherson's Printing Group

National Library of Australia
Cataloguing-in-Publication data:
McLellan, Betty, 1938– .
    Help! I'm living with a (man) boy.
    ISBN 9781876756628 (pbk).
    ISBN 1 876756 62 4 (pbk).
    1. Interpersonal relations. 2. Man-woman relationships. I. Title.

302

Contents

Boy-power

Can't live with him, can't live without him

Introduction

When I was young, I was such a romantic. I was convinced I was going to meet a wonderful man. We would both fall madly in love, get married, have three beautiful children and "live happily ever after". Now, after fourteen years of marriage, the reality is I'm on my own with four children. One of them is my husband.

This was how one woman described her experience to a group of women as they sat around discussing their relationships with men. Others in the group spoke of similar experiences.

In my work with women over many years, one fact has remained constant. In situations where women feel free to speak honestly about their relationships, many express deep disappointment and frustration, the cause of which is very often identified as the absence of adult companionship.

He's just like a child. If he doesn't get his own way, he throws a tantrum.

If I say "no" when he wants sex, he sulks for days. It's just not worth it.

He does his own thing most of the time . . . doesn't contribute anything socially or emotionally to the family . . . seems to prefer to be with his mates. But, when it suits him to have the kids and I go somewhere with him, we have to show immense interest and excitement, otherwise he loses it and starts to throw his weight around.

This theme of men's immaturity in relationships is a very common one in discussions among women. What it reveals is that while men, in general, may be quite happy with their lives, many women are not. For many women, the quality of companionship and emotional involvement they get from men leaves a lot to be desired. So, the obvious question is: what can be done to address the imbalance which exists in relationships in terms of emotional satisfaction?

If you are a woman living with a man who is a "boy", I'm sure you have tried just about everything to get him to change, including kidding to him, coaxing him, humouring him, cuddling up to him, getting angry with him, threatening to leave him—all to no avail in any long-term sense. What can you do? The very first thing you must do, I believe, is stand back and look at what is actually going on between the two of you. What is he doing? What are you doing? That's what this book is about. This is my attempt to help women begin to examine the dynamics of their relationships. I admit it isn't an easy thing to do, but it is definitely worth the trouble. It may well result in a better relationship and a happier life for both of you.

The purpose of this book

In writing this book, I have a very clear and simple purpose: to inject some much-needed honesty into our thinking about relationships between immature men and the women who struggle to relate to them.* My purpose of honesty is achieved in two ways. First, the situations I

---

* I could also write about relationships between immature women and the men who struggle to relate to them. They do exist. But, because of the number of women who share their pain with me in therapy, I choose here to focus on the immaturity of men and the damaging effect their behaviour has on their partners.

have chosen for discussion contain honest and straight-forward descriptions of the harmful and destructive behaviour which usually accompanies emotional imma-turity in men. An examination of the society in which we live shows that there is a much greater emphasis on a man's right to individual freedom than on the need for men to develop a sense of responsibility to others. The result is that there exists, in modern society, a real reluct-ance to hold men accountable for their bad behaviour toward anybody and, particularly, toward women. There exists also a compulsion to excuse and forgive men, no matter what they do. One of the things I do in this book is focus on the kinds of immature behaviour that men get away with, and say "enough is enough".

The other way my purpose of honesty is achieved is to include in all the situations honest and straightforward descriptions of the effect men's emotional immaturity has on the women closest to them. Most women in such situations have little realisation of the degree of strain they are under, of the way their personalities are being affected, or of the sense of loss and emptiness they live with day after day. With this as the central focus of the book, it is my hope that women will begin to question the value of sacrificing their entire lives in the vain hope that their partner (who, in all probability, does not want to change and has no intention of changing) may one day change. It is my hope that women will see value in their own lives and will find more positive things to do with their time and energy than going endlessly around in circles trying to satisfy the demands of immature men.

The need for honesty

The social and psychological health of any society depends upon its citizens' willingness to look at the dynamics that exist in all kinds of relationships: between women and men, rich and poor, indigenous and nonindigenous, politicians and the people they represent. In regard to relationships between the sexes, the mental health and happiness of both women and men depend upon their willingness to look honestly at the dynamics that exist between them, with a view to changing anything that needs to be changed.

To pretend that the immature behaviour indulged in by a great number of men is not really happening, or that there is some cause over which they have no control, is to do a great disservice to those men as well as to the women (and children) affected by their behaviour. It allows such men to go on avoiding the truth about themselves and their attitudes to women, and to go on behaving in ways that destroy their own potential for integrity. When a man is not held accountable for his behaviour and attitudes, he is robbed of the opportunity to change. Also, the opportunity for the women involved to enjoy mental health and happiness is severely affected. Women living with immature men whose behaviour is regularly excused by this and that rationalisation often feel confused, isolated, guilty and "crazy".

The mental health of any society requires that the truth about relationships between the sexes be exposed so that all citizens have the freedom to make decisions about their own happiness *based on the facts*. If a man is told clearly by society that his immature behaviour is unacceptable, then he is free to make a decision about whether or not he wants to continue behaving in that way. His choice is clear. When he is not given that message, when his bad behaviour is continually defended or excused, he is given room to think his behaviour is not offensive. Honesty and integrity demand that society give him the opportunity to make a choice based on clear feedback about his behaviour.

Similarly, when a woman is in possession of the facts about the immaturity of her partner's behaviour, she is able to see her situation more clearly and make informed decisions about her future.

Achieving the goal of honesty

In the writing of this book, I have felt enormous pressure to be "nice", to present immature men and their behaviour as "not so bad" and to share the blame around by making a point of the fact that "women are immature too". That this pressure has come from inside myself has confirmed for me how deeply ingrained in all of us is the desire to excuse men. We want to believe that deep down inside, these men are not really as self-centred or childish as their behaviour indicates. Unfortunately, the experience of many women reveals that they are.

Similarly, I have resisted the temptation to minimise the effect that men's immature behaviour has on women. I realise it would have been far less stressful for me if I had chosen to write in a more positive vein, presenting a picture of the strengths women develop in such trying circumstances. But to scratch around to find a few positives to say about an overwhelmingly negative situation would be dishonest in the extreme. I am convinced that the road to more mature and satisfying relationships begins with honesty about how things actually are.

The book's goal of honesty does not end with my own honesty as an author. It is my hope that individual men and women will be inspired, through the pages of this book, toward a greater degree of honesty within themselves about their own situations. I also hope that the pursuit of such honesty will lead them to the kind of personal maturity that will allow them to enjoy the give and take that constitutes a relationship based on genuine love, respect and equality.

- *For men,* the purpose will have been achieved if it helps immature men stop and examine their attitudes toward women; acknowledge their need for a better understanding of their own emotions; admit the ease with which they take out their frustrations on the women closest to them; acknowledge the injustice of the situation they have created; and begin to change.

- *For women,* the purpose will have been achieved if it helps them open their eyes to what is really happening in their relationships; decide to stop using up so much energy trying to infuse maturity into a man who prefers to be immature; stop blaming themselves for a situation that is not their fault; gain a greater understanding of their own feelings of disappointment and emptiness and loneliness; and begin to look at their options for a better future.

What is it about men?

Poor men. I suppose we ought to feel sorry for them to some extent. In every generation, you see, men are sold a lie. In their socialisation, they are deceived into believing that they are superior and that their superiority gives them unlimited power over women, animals, the environment, material goods, and all the world's wealth. With men who are white, the lie goes even further to include superiority over men and women of every other race. It's all a lie. But let's not waste too much energy feeling sorry for them, because this is a lie that most men are glad to accept as fact. They find it too attractive to resist. They like the power it gives them. It enables them to see themselves as life's winners. And they have no intention of giving up the privileges their "superior" position affords them.

While women and other disempowered groups have suffered because of the way "superior" white males treat them, there is a sense in which that suffering has brought a greater awareness of ourselves and a more enhanced ability to relate to others. The very survival of oppressed people depends on their ability to adjust to and appease their oppressor. That this dynamic operates in relationships goes some way toward explaining why women, in every generation, have worked hard at learning how to relate to men, while men have mostly not bothered. There is an immaturity about the attitudes and behaviour of many men in their relationships with women and a continuing attempt by women to adjust to that immaturity. Such a negative situation fails to bring happiness to either partner.

It is my wish that the reverse were true, that men would see the maturity which exists in the attitudes and behaviour of most women, and work on themselves to match that level of maturity.

Are all men immature?

No. All men are not immature. Thankfully, there are many men who manage to counter the socialisation into arrogance and self-centredness that seems to be standard for males in most countries of the world. The myth of the superiority of men teaches boys that women exist to cater to men's needs and that women are not important in the great scheme of things. A woman's opinions, intuitions, feelings and desires are considered important only to the extent that they interact with or relate to the opinions, intuitions, feelings and desires of a man. Those women who insist on being responded to as people in their own right are discounted as having nothing useful to offer.

It is not altogether clear how some men escape or counter normal socialisation to become fair and decent human beings, but the fact remains that it does happen. Mature men demonstrate that they are not afraid to relate to women as equals. They are not afraid of women's power, women's intelligence, women's abilities, women's sexuality and, consequently, feel no need to subsume women's attributes under their own. Also, men of maturity have no difficulty acknowledging that women are oppressed in a male-privileged society, speaking out against that oppression, and working alongside women to bring about change.

Are men the only ones who behave in an emotionally immature way?

No. Some women, also, behave in an emotionally immature way, and it is usually their partners who suffer the effects of their oppressive behaviour.

There will be those who will criticise this book's one-sidedness and insist that, in the name of fairness, I should have told both sides of the story. It is not fair, they will say, to pick on men by highlighting their immaturity, when women can be immature too. I agree that the book is one-sided, and intentionally so, but I do not agree with the suggestion that both sides of the story ought to have been presented equally. All such an equal presentation would do is cancel out the guilt of all guilty parties.

In the interests of psychological health, as well as ethical integrity, it is crucial that each situation of injustice be dealt with separately so that one is not allowed simply to cancel out the other. When everyone is said to be equally guilty, no one is guilty, and nothing is resolved. The immaturity of men and the immaturity of women are two separate issues and must be dealt with separately in order that solid progress can be made toward healthier and more satisfying relationships.

What's a woman to do?

If it is true, as this book suggests, that emotional immaturity in men is commonplace, what is a woman to do? When her relationship is tearing her apart and turning her into the kind of person she never wanted to be—frustrated, complaining, bitter, depressed—what choices does she have? It has long been thought that a woman living with an immature man had only two choices: either to stay and put up with it, or to leave. Women's experiences, however, reveal that there are at least two more choices available. They are: to stay and make the best of a bad situation, or to stay but develop emotional independence.

Stay and put up with it

Of the four options available, this first one is the least desirable because it is the most psychologically and emotionally damaging. The decision to stay and put up with it seems to belong to another era but, sadly, it is the decision still made today by many women who feel they have no other option. The pressure on women to stay in relationships with immature men, even when those men are violent or intimidating or sexually unfaithful, is enormous. The opinions of parents, children, friends and the church, the absence of community support, the fear of poverty, fear of being alone, fear of the unknown, fear of a sense of failing, all add up to a huge amount of pressure to stay with the devil you know.

For many women, though, the decision to stay and put up with it is, in fact, a decision to live as non-persons. It means surrendering their right to have opinions, to have their own friends, to express emotions, to be engaged in work that is satisfying, to dream their own dreams, to plan for their future. A non-person is one who is not real, a false person. Anything about such a woman that is potentially real is swallowed up by the demands and expectations of the immature man who is her partner. It is usually true that a woman in this situation does not give herself over to falseness because of any *desire* to be false, any desire to lose herself, any desire to give up the lively, energetic, spontaneous woman she may have once been but because, at some level, she knows that this is the relationship's only chance for survival. While not fully understanding it, she senses that her partner, in some way, feeds on the life he crushes out of her. She senses that he needs to keep her down in order to keep himself up. When, knowing all this, she still cannot find it within herself to leave, she must settle for what little joy she can find within the limits he allows.*

Leave the relationship

The second of the four options is to leave the relationship. This is the best advice anyone can give to a woman in a relationship with a man whose attitudes and behaviour reduce the woman to nothing and who shows absolutely no interest in negotiating a change. If you are in a situation like that, my advice to you is to leave— now. This is not to say that leaving is easy, but it is sometimes a necessity. If you are living with a man who is physically and/or emotionally destructive and the situation shows no sign of changing, plan your escape carefully and then do it. Do it for your own sake and for the sake of your children if you have them.

As you plan, however, be aware that the fury of a man who has one of his possessions taken away can be fierce. Your leaving deprives him of that which he believes he "owns". Also, your leaving deprives him of his "right" to debase and degrade you and, without

---

* While a woman in this situation may survive physically and materially (and even that cannot be guaranteed), she does so at great cost to her emotional and spiritual health, as well as to her sense of self.

anyone to debase and degrade, his life is in danger of losing its meaning. His reaction could be extreme and it is naïve not to be prepared for that possibility, so when you plan your escape, do so with your eyes wide open to all the possible consequences.

The experience of most women living with immature men, on the other hand, is that their situation is not totally negative. It is frustrating much of the time, but there are some good times in among the bad. Although the good times do not make the bad times acceptable, they nevertheless make the idea of leaving a little more complicated.* Women in these situations spend a great deal of time struggling with thoughts of how they might stay in their relationship without simply "putting up with it".

Stay and make the best of a bad situation

One way of staying without simply "putting up with it" is the third option mentioned above. To stay and make the best of a bad situation is actually the option recommended by most authors of popular self-help literature on relationships and, consequently, is the option chosen by the many women who place their hope in the strategies contained in those books. If a woman is able to convince herself that her partner's bad behaviour is

---

* Sometimes a woman will allow herself to drift along in such a relationship until she meets and falls in love with someone else. While it may seem easier, or more legitimate, to leave for another man than to leave to preserve one's own self-respect, such a strategy is not recommended because it has the effect of allowing both partners to avoid confronting the real reason for the breakdown in their relationship. This means that both partners will move into future relationships with unresolved issues which will, more than likely, have a negative effect on their new relationships.

actually "alien" behaviour and, therefore, not to be taken seriously, if she can see his behaviour as "cute", if she can trivialise his behaviour, if she can be "understanding" and "forgiving", then she may be able to make the best of it.

While this option is much better than the first option, it must be remembered that the advice to "stay and make the best of it" is still degrading of women. It actually invites women to degrade themselves by pretending the bad behaviour perpetrated against them is "not so bad".

Stay but develop emotional independence

A better option for those who cannot bring themselves to walk away from a relationship which causes them constant pain and distress, is the final one mentioned above, which is to work at developing emotional independence. The value of this option is that it provides a way for women in these situations to avoid being hurt all the time.

Motivated by an acute sense of justice and a belief that justice and fairness will prevail in the end, many women fight ongoing battles in their relationships, battles which they are certain they will eventually win but which use up an enormous amount of energy along the way. The result of women's persistence combined with men's resistance is usually that a relationship becomes stuck in a rut that just grows deeper and deeper.

Take the common example of the wet towel on the bathroom floor. Women who live with men who persist in leaving their wet towels in a heap on the bathroom floor usually tie themselves up in emotional knots over the injustice involved in that one act. They are right, of course. It is unjust when one adult has to walk around after another adult performing menial tasks on that person's behalf just to keep their shared environment liveable. But one has to question the value of women engaging in the same unwinnable battle every day of their lives.

The first thing an emotionally independent woman must do is admit to herself that her partner has already demonstrated that there are some behaviours he will never change. Once you admit that to yourself, you will pull right back on those issues. You will stop using up your emotional energy trying to get him to change things he has already decided not to change. That is the only sensible course to take.

Such battles are difficult to give up, though, because giving up on issues of justice is the same as giving in and allowing injustice to win. There is much more at stake than justice, too. While you continue to work on your partner to pick up his wet towel (or whatever other issues you are having to contend with), you are able to believe there is still hope; but once you give up the fight, it can feel as if you have given up hope. When hope is all we have to hold on to, when hope is what sustains us and gives us a reason to continue trying in the face of constant disappointment, it is no small matter to decide to let it go. When a woman can let go of her fragile hope and focus instead on the reality of her situation, though, her feelings of desperation, frustration and bitterness are usually replaced with a new hope, a hope based on reality rather than wishful thinking. Accepting the way things are, allows you to become unstuck, to get out of the rut. You will then begin to look honestly at your relationship and make decisions for the future based on that honesty.

Before making the decision to create emotional distance, it is always important for a woman to give her relationship one last chance to be the kind of partnership she has always wanted. Make one last attempt, an unemotional attempt, to speak to your partner about negotiating some changes in the ways you relate to each other. If your partner responds with interest and involvement, then there is hope for a closer, more cooperative relationship in the future. If, on the other hand, he ignores or ridicules or gets angry at you, then you must begin making plans either to leave him or to develop emotional independence. The value of emotional distance, or emotional independence, is that you can still enjoy the good parts of the relationship while saving yourself from much of the unnecessary hurt and pain. Of course, you may still be picking up his wet towel (!), but you will not allow yourself to be emotionally distraught over it. Instead of resenting the fact that you have to pick up after your partner, you will choose to interpret it as doing something for yourself, to satisfy your own need to meet certain standards of tidiness in the bathroom. Incidentally, if your aim is to win "the battle of the wet towel", this way of dealing with it will sound like a cop-out, but if your aim is to develop a degree of emotional independence, then achieving a situation where you are not emotionally devastated by your partner's thoughtless actions day after day will be very satisfying.

What does emotional independence mean? It does not mean you will become "cold" or "hard", although you will probably be accused of that. Whenever women decide to take a different attitude toward their partner's cruel or thoughtless behaviour and stop being hurt by it, a different power dynamic begins to emerge, and immature men resent the change. It makes them feel less powerful, less dominant, and it is not uncommon to see men lash out physically or verbally in an attempt to restore the old power dynamic.

Also, emotional independence does not mean total independence. It does not mean you will begin doing your own thing without regard for your responsibilities, without regard for the feelings and wishes of those closest to you. It does not mean you will become self-absorbed and uncooperative.

Again, it does not necessarily mean you will be physically and sexually distant from your partner. When you *want* to be close or when you *want* to make love, there is no reason not to. The relationship will continue and, in fact, has the potential to be much more enjoyable once you learn how to create the emotional space that stops you feeling all the hurt you used to feel.

So, what is emotional independence? *Emotional independence is the ability to distance oneself from one's own emotions.* Although the end result will be that emotional distance is created between you and your partner's hurtful words and actions, the way to achieve that is to create distance, not between yourself and your partner, but between yourself and your own emotions. How does that work, in practical terms? Begin by standing back from any situation which has the potential to devastate you. Objectify it. Push it away from you and observe it. In other words, practise making your response a head-level response rather than an emotional response. In this way, you create the distance needed to protect yourself from your own feelings of hurt.*

---

* This option is not to be interpreted as favouring a rational response to situations over an emotional response. Indeed, it must not be forgotten that the reason this option of creating emotional distance has become necessary is because so many men refuse, or are unable, to respond emotionally when that is the appropriate response. For women to train themselves to become as emotionally inept as immature men are would be a huge backward step. The aim of this option is to encourage women to learn the skill of creating emotional space and to use such a strategy only when it is needed to protect themselves from ongoing hurtful situations.

Of the four options available to women in relationships with immature men, the second and fourth described above are the options most worthy of consideration. If your partner refuses to consider growing up and
becoming an adult, then leaving him is a very sensible
and life-affirming option. For those women who prefer
not to leave, the option of developing emotional independence is recommended as the best alternative because
it, also, has the potential to be life-affirming.

The structure of the book

This book is structured in such a way as to allow readers
to choose whatever they want to read. There is much to
be gained in terms of consistency and flow from reading
the piece as a whole, but it is also possible to take from
the book whatever one finds immediately relevant.

The forty-one practical situations which follow
highlight the serious effect men's immature attitudes and
behaviour have on the women with whom they live. Each
of the scenarios contains a discussion of the issues
involved and most include down-to-earth suggestions for
action. Above all, women are encouraged to see hope in
standing firm and insisting on their right to share their
lives with men who are mature adults.

Everyday situations

1. When you want some answers

If it's answers you want, read on. Although answers are not exactly laid out for you, there are plenty of suggestions designed to help you find your own answers to problems experienced in relationships with immature men.

In most of the situations you are about to read, you will find:

- a description of the situation,
- a broader analysis or discussion, and
- some suggestions for action.

Some of the situations are dealt with very briefly and others in more detail. Some are dealt with in a fairly light way while others are given much more serious treatment. This is done partly for variety and partly as a way of demonstrating the fact that women who choose to stay in distressing relationships will only survive adequately if they learn to respond to their situation in two ways. At one level, the distressing aspects of the relationship must be taken seriously, but at another level they can and ought to be laughed at.

Of the hundreds of situations that could have been chosen for discussion, why did I choose this particular selection of forty-one? They seemed to me to be among the most common situations experienced by the women I've met. Some readers will find every one of the situations familiar while others will find only some that resonate with their own experiences. Whatever your own situation is, I hope you find the discussions interesting and helpful.

As mentioned above, I have not actually attempted to give answers to the problems raised because it would be somewhat arrogant of me to presume I had answers to all the concerns of women living with immature men.

However, it is my hope that the suggestions for action will help readers discover their own answers and the courage to put their discoveries into practice.

So, if you want to find your own answers, if you want to improve your self-esteem, if you want to grow stronger and more courageous, if you want to have relationships that are more real and, therefore more satisfying, read on . . .

Men are such boys

2. When the man in your life is a child

Remember how much you looked forward to meeting the man of your dreams? According to the stereotype you grew up with, he would be older than you, taller than you, stronger than you. He would earn more money than you. He would love and cherish you. He would be prepared to lay down his life to protect you and the children you had jointly brought into the world.

Most women enter into marriage, or long-term commitment, consciously or unconsciously believing they are taking the first step toward the fulfilment of such a dream. Their commitment is to sharing their lives with another adult which, they anticipate, will include discussing things together, laughing, playing, enjoying each other's company, loving each other, negotiating, working together to ensure fairness and justice for both of them as well as their offspring. For some women, it does proceed in that way, but for others there is an early and devastating jolt. The reality is that the man of their dreams has turned out to be a "child".

What does that mean? What is a man–child actually like? To understand the man–child phenomenon, it is necessary to look, first, at the attitudes and behaviour of children generally, and then to place one of those children in a man's body, with all the power and privileges that come with being an adult male. The result can be frightening.

Young children are usually very egocentric. In other words, their whole world revolves around themselves and their needs. When babies are hungry, they demand attention by crying until their need is satisfied. When young children want attention, they make a fuss until they get the attention they are looking for. When angry, they may lash out at others. When frustrated, they may throw tantrums. When unable to get their own way, they may withdraw and sulk. (Does any of this sound familiar?) All such immature responses are perfectly natural and understandable in young children because immature responses are normal in those who have not had time to mature. In adults, however, such behaviour is unacceptable.

It is expected that a child who develops in a normal, healthy way will gradually become aware that there are other people in the world who also have needs and whose needs are as legitimate as their own. In most children, this maturing does not occur automatically but comes about with the help and guidance and example of significant adults.

The fact that some children miss out on such maturing can be attributed to one or more of the following reasons: First, some parents fail to provide their children with the tools they need to help them develop into mature adults because they, as parents, do not possess that ability themselves. Second, many well-meaning parents who do have the ability to guide their children, choose not to because they live by the philosophy that children should be allowed the freedom to be who they want to be. Parents are urged by this philosophy to be careful not to take away their children's autonomy by attempting to pass on their own values to their children. Religion is one such value. Since the 1970s, it has been common to hear parents say: "I'm not going to push religion on to my children. When they're old enough, they can decide for themselves." Simple manners is another value. Confronted with a child's rudeness and lack of respect for others, many parents say nothing in the belief that it is not their place to sanction their children.

Such a view is a curious one, given that values never develop in a vacuum. If children do not get the basis for their own value system from their parents, they will get it from television, computer games, friends or other adults. Children need someone else's value system to interact with so that they have a starting-point when struggling to sort out their own values. Some will simply adopt their parents' values as they are, but most will either adjust those values to suit themselves or rebel against them and develop a totally new system of their own. Parents who choose not to offer guidance, not to impose some structure, are leaving their children to flounder.

A third reason behind the failure of some children to grow into mature adults is that parents and other adults find them too difficult to handle and abandon attempts to guide them toward more acceptable behaviour. Aggressive boys, in particular, are often allowed free rein because the drama involved in trying to discipline them or encourage them to develop respect for people and property is too stressful and disruptive for other members of the family. This is not said as a criticism of parents, many of whom try everything they know before finally giving up. Rather, it is an observation of a situation in which the development of responsible attitudes and behaviour seems almost impossible.

A further reason for the failure of some children to develop maturity in adulthood, and probably the most common, is the example of the same-sex parent. Many girls learn from the self-defeating behaviour of their mothers to be passive and dependent and devious and dissatisfied and complaining. They learn to limit themselves and their expectations. They learn how to settle for much less than they would like. They learn to make do with unsatisfactory relationships. They learn to blame themselves when things go wrong.

Many boys learn from the example of their fathers that the way to stay in control in life is to be arrogant and self-centred. They learn that the aim is to win, and that the way to win is to make sure those around them lose. They learn, also, that to show any emotion, or to take account of how others feel, is weak. The only people worthy of respect are those who are physically stronger or socially and financially more powerful than themselves. Boys learn from such fathers that women are to be given no respect. A man can joke with women, tease them, poke them, maul them, but never have a serious, adult conversation with them. They can be ignored, ridiculed, intimidated, even assaulted, because what women think is not centrally important to his life. A boy who grows up to be a man–child is often following the example of the man–child who was his father.

When a child who has never learnt mature responses, grows into a man with a man's body, a man's sexual urges and a man's physical strength, combined with all the privileges, all the favoured treatment society affords men, the result can be extremely difficult for those around him. It is not surprising that those who usually bear the brunt of the man–child phenomenon are women and children.

What can be done about this phenomenon? I often hear concerned women say that the way to change the situation of immaturity in men is to start with little boys. Train boys to be different, they say, and start from the moment they are born. Whenever I hear this "solution" being expounded, it is usually said as if no one has ever thought of it before and, also, as if it would be certain to bring about change in men in the space of one generation. The reality is that it has been thought of before. Brilliant minds in the field of education have been working in this area for a long time, but all acknowledge that progress is slow. A major reason for the slow progress is that while educators are working with children to change attitudes between the sexes, overwhelmingly negative adult influences still exist all around them. Boys are still presented every day with images of dominant, macho men. Most violence on television, whether on the news, in sports coverage or in movies, is perpetrated by men. Most computer games are about men competing with each other, with one eventually prevailing over all the others. On the home front, it is common for men to be absent, to be absorbed in their own interests and therefore withdrawn from the family, or to be just plain difficult.

While it is important that educators and parents continue working with children with a view to changing gender stereotypes and expectations, the attitudes and behaviour of adult men must also be targeted. There must be increasing pressure brought to bear on men to change the culture of masculinity so that the culture into which boys are socialised enables them to develop into adults who are mature, sensitive, decent human beings.

Suggestions for action

What can individual women do when the man they live with is a child? The following suggestions may be helpful.

Don't look for ways to excuse him

When a woman is distressed about her partner's immature attitudes and behaviour, it is natural that she will think about her situation and try to figure out why he behaves as he does, but it is important not to become obsessive about it. Most women who live with difficult men spend an inordinate amount of time thinking, analysing, looking for explanations for their partner's behaviour. Some actually admit that they think of nothing else.

The influence of Freud and psychoanalysis on Western societies is such that thinking women and men immediately, almost automatically, look for underlying causes when confronted with unusual or anti-social behaviour. There is nothing wrong with that. In fact, it is quite helpful to seek a fuller picture, to try to see a person's behaviour in a broader context, but the danger is that excessive probing into the past can also have the effect of distorting the reality of the present. The most common outcome is that the past provides "excuses" for behaviour which, in the present, is inexcusable.

When probing into anyone's childhood, it is fairly easy to "discover" events and relationships that were problematic for the child and that could be the basis for ongoing personality problems. A woman searching for clues to explain her partner's immature and unacceptable behaviour will find just that—clues, possible explanations, possible contributing factors. He may, as a child, have been neglected by his mother. He may have been abandoned by his father when he was a baby. He may have been sexually abused by the man down the road. He may, as a young man, have fought in the Vietnam war. He may have been betrayed by his first wife. He may feel trapped in a job he hates. A woman's probing may uncover any or all of the above, but they are still only "possible contributing factors". They are not excuses. Whatever may have happened to a man in his childhood or in his early adult years, it does not provide an excuse for current bad behaviour. Like every adult, it is incumbent upon him to recognise the connection between his present behaviour and his earlier experiences and make a determined effort to work through those earlier traumas, either by himself or with a therapist. If he refuses to do that, it is because he is not interested enough in changing his present behaviour. Such indifference cannot be excused.

Don't feel sorry for him

A woman who delves into her partner's background in a desperate attempt to find an explanation for his bad behaviour, will often go one step further than excusing him. She turns it all around and finds a way to feel sorry for him. Even though he is the perpetrator and she is his victim, *she* feels sorry for *him*. She sees him as a poor unfortunate one who had a difficult childhood and now "can't help himself". Women in these situations must understand that excusing such a man and feeling sorry for him only provides him with the excuse to continue his offending behaviour.

Stay true to yourself

Women who struggle to survive in their relationships with immature men testify to the fact that it is sometimes difficult to keep a grip on reality. It is sometimes difficult to remember who they are and to stay true to themselves. It is difficult to trust their own thoughts and opinions when they are told constantly that they have no idea what they are talking about. It is difficult to stay in touch with their emotions when their emotions are constantly ridiculed. It is difficult to believe in their own sanity when they are constantly told they are mad. It is difficult to maintain belief in themselves when who they are, what they say, how they speak, what they look like and what they achieve are continually criticised.

If you are one of those women who have chosen to stay in such a relationship, you must pay attention to your own needs so that you can stay strong within yourself. You must find the strength to believe in yourself and stay true to yourself. In the same way that negative input on a continuing basis has a damaging effect on one's self-esteem, positive input from others bolsters one's self-esteem. It is crucial, therefore, that women in relationships with immature men make sure they have regular contact with friends who care about them, so that the positive feedback they receive balances out the negative they receive from their partner.

Create some emotional distance*

Women, much more than men, see marriage or long-term relationships as requiring total emotional commitment at all times. In such circumstances, a woman is committed to being there for her partner no matter how difficult he may be and no matter how indifferent he may be to her needs. In other words, she makes herself vulnerable. She lays herself open to be hurt by his attitudes and behaviour.

It is true that loving someone usually does involve trust and a willingness to be vulnerable, but in a situation where one partner's trust is regularly betrayed by the other, continued vulnerability can only be counter-productive.

If you are a woman who has decided, for your own reasons, to stay in a relationship which causes you a high degree of emotional pain and distress on a continuing basis, you must engage in some kind of protective behaviour. It is simply foolish for you to remain open and vulnerable when you know, from past experiences, that you will be let down again and again. What do I mean by "protective behaviour"? I suggest that, if there are areas

---

* This is the strategy which leads to emotional independence. See Introduction, pp. 12–15.

[Postcard] Jacky Fleming (1992).
When I grow up. Leeds: Leeds Postcards.

of the relationship that are reasonably good, you invest
your energy in those areas, but *withdraw your emotional
investment from those areas where you are caused most
pain.* If one does not have an emotional investment in a
situation, that situation has far less power to hurt and
destroy.

For example, if you and your partner enjoy working
together in the garden and there is a degree of closeness
in that environment, then enjoy that experience. Be
emotionally involved with him during those activities.
But, at other times, when he is rude or dismissive or
abusive, develop the ability to create emotional distance.
If he makes a habit of putting you down in front of your
friends, for example, be prepared for it. Make up your
mind that next time he does it, you will not cringe. You
will not be crushed. You will not feel embarrassed. In
fact, you will not let your feelings engage in any way. You

will be dispassionate. Simply stand back from it and observe it ("He's doing it again"), respond to it in your own head ("That's typical") and get on with enjoying the evening with your friends.

When you develop this ability to respond at a head level rather than an emotional level in such instances, you will find it becomes easier to allow your partner's immature remarks to flow right over you. This is not to suggest you *accept* his immaturity but, rather, that you train yourself not to be affected by it. If you choose to stay in a difficult relationship, then creating emotional distance, when required, is an important form of self-protection.

3. When you feel like his mother

Most women, looking forward to entering into long-term relationships with men, do have a dream that theirs will be a reasonably equal partnership. Every woman who gives it any thought wants to believe that she will marry, or live with, a man who has a mature attitude toward life and with whom she can have an adult–adult relationship. The reality is, however, that many end up in parent–child relationships.

In my psychotherapy practice over the years, count-less women have expressed disappointment in themselves that they, all too often, hear themselves "sounding like his mother". Of course, there are women who enjoy being the dominant partner but the majority, it seems, would prefer a situation of peaceful equality. When one looks at the socialisation of women and men in Western cultures, though, it becomes clear that equality is almost an impossible dream.

To begin with, many of the roles expected of women in their relationships are mothering or nurturing roles. The expectation, in most households, continues to be that the woman will wash and iron her partner's clothes, cook and serve his food, and clean up after him.* The woman will listen endlessly and patiently to her partner's worries about his work. She will counsel him and nurture him. She will compliment him, boost his spirits and make him feel better about his potential for success.

In line with the civilising effect women are supposed to have on men, she will accept the task of trying to make him a better person. This involves setting an example for

---

* Some couples have worked together at developing a more equal distribution of household tasks, but the majority still persist in following the old stereotypes.

him in a variety of situations. To focus on a common point of contention, a woman may attempt to set an example for her partner by picking up the clothes he leaves lying around wherever he steps out of them. And when he seems a little slow at catching on to her example, she will take it a step further and begin patiently *asking* him to pick up his clothes. When he does pick them up, she will praise him, even thank him, in the hope that it will reinforce his "good" behaviour. Then, when his clothes are left on the floor the following day, she will ask patiently again. And the next day. And the next day.

All of the above is mothering behaviour—washing, ironing, cooking, cleaning, listening, counselling, nurturing, praising, teaching, training—and it is the kind of behaviour society expects women to engage in, not just in relation to their children but also in relation to their partners.

The other side of the coin from the "maternal woman" is the "individual man", the expectation being that, while a woman exists for others, a man exists for himself. The "individual man" must prove his individuality by resisting, refusing to cooperate, and generally frustrating his partner's attempts at developing an adult–adult relationship. Since the parent–child dynamic works to men's advantage and to women's detriment, it is no wonder that women's attempts to change that dynamic are so often met with fierce resistance.

Although it involves something of a contradiction, it seems that the "individual man" likes the dynamic between the maternal woman and the man–child and the tactic of resistance is designed to ensure there is no change in the status quo. As every woman could testify, there are men everywhere, not just in personal relationships but also in social and work situations, who are masters of the art of resistance. They resist hearing. They resist answering. They resist any kind of response that might give the person speaking to them a clue about how, or if, they have received the message. An interesting point to note is that this tactic of resistance is not generally used against everyone. It is usually only employed when the person wanting a response is the man's wife or girl-friend, his mother, or a woman with whom he works (either as a colleague or a client). This discriminatory aspect of his resistance proves that his behaviour is delib-erate and, as such, is extremely frustrating for the victim.

What often happens in a relationship is that a woman who is ignored tries harder. She begins by being assertive, which is a normal healthy way for adults to communicate but, when her attempts at communication are ignored, she tries different tactics in the hope of getting a response. The more she tries, the more he ignores her. The more her attempts are ignored, the more frustrated she becomes until, finally, she explodes. She becomes aggressive. Many women speak of the disap-pointment they feel when they hear themselves "out of control"—yelling, screaming, crying. Often such extreme expressions do get results but any response from a man in these situations is usually reluctant and resentful and, altogether, the whole scenario does nothing to improve the relationship. He resents her outburst and she feels badly about herself for having resorted to such aggressive tactics. He resents being treated like a child and she hates herself for sounding like a domineering mother. And it all started with his resistance to her need for an adult–adult relationship.

Suggestions for action

How is it possible to avoid feeling like your partner's mother, whether a loving, nurturing mother or a loud, domineering mother?

Develop an awareness of the way society trains women
for the mother role

It is general knowledge, these days, that there is nothing incidental about the fact that little girls are encouraged to play with dolls. Most of us are now aware that this is society's way of socialising girls into the adult role of motherhood. When we received our first doll, we had to learn how to care for our "baby". We learnt how to hold our dolls, feed them, dress them, comfort them, heal their wounds. We learnt that it was necessary to sacrifice our own comfort to attend to their every need. If a little girl did that, she would sometimes be rewarded by being told that she was "a good mother".

This awareness of the way we are socialised from a young age to care for babies, however, is really only part of the story. The fact is that little girls with their dolls are actually in training to mother everybody! And so we do. Throughout our lives, we mother our babies, our children, our partners, our friends, our ageing parents.

From now on, whenever you find yourself thinking about your relationship with your partner and pondering on why it is that you so easily slip into the mother role, let me suggest you consider your socialisation. All of those caring things (mentioned above) which you learnt to do for your dolls, are exactly the things you are expected to do for your partner: care for him, hold him, feed him, prepare his clothes, comfort him, heal his wounds and sacrifice your own comfort to attend to his every need. You may not enjoy it but, the fact is, you find yourself doing it. You may even resent it, but to break away from that which you have been socialised to do would take a tremendous effort of will.

[Postcard] © Flying Fish, Inglewood (US).

Think of yourself as an adult (not a parent)

What I suggest is that you make that "tremendous effort of will" and break away from the conditioning of your socialisation. Be determined that the only people you will be a parent to are the children entrusted to your care, or other adults whom you willingly care for in times of crisis. You are not your partner's mother. You are the adult who shares his life. If he wants mothering on a day-to-day basis, he will have to do it for himself.*

---

* I do not mean to imply that there is no room for nurturing in a loving relationship. Indeed, mutual nurturing is an important aspect of any caring adult relationship. It is when the nurturing is totally one-sided, as in a parent–child dynamic, that it must change.

Breaking out of one's conditioning is difficult but not impossible if you take the following steps:

- Open yourself up to knowledge about the conditioning process, as suggested above. Allow yourself to see that you act in certain ways and hold certain views because your socialisation has made those behaviours and attitudes seem "natural".

- Be prepared to question the value of your present behaviours and attitudes. There will be some you will want to keep and some you will want to change.

- Take each of those behaviours you would like to change, and develop a clear picture of the way you would prefer to be.

- Develop new ways of behaving in line with your new preferences.

- Practise each new behaviour until you feel comfortable with it. Be aware that until a new behaviour becomes "natural", there will be a strong pull back to your socialisation. Old habits can be changed, but only by practising new behaviours which become new habits to take the place of the old.

What will this mean for you, then, in the context of your relationship? First, you will allow yourself to see that, as a woman, you have been conditioned into a mothering role in relation to your partner. Then, you will question the value of continuing the parent–child dynamic that exists between you. Of course, if it works for both of you, if you are both happy with the relationship as it is, then you may choose to continue but, if one of you would like more out of the relationship, then begin to develop a picture of what it would be like for you if you stopped playing the mother role. Talk with your partner about the changes you are intending to make. Then, practise relating as an adult. Replace the old mothering behaviour with that of a reasonable adult. How will you do that?

If the morning routine in your household is a problem to you, then that would be a good place to start. Mature men—that is, those who engage in normal adult behaviour—usually take responsibility for the way their day begins, but others expect or allow their wives to take total responsibility for waking them up, coaxing them out of bed, preparing their breakfast, and continually reminding them of the time so as to ensure that they are not late for work. If that is a description of your situation, it is time for a change. Begin by telling your partner that you intend making changes to the morning routine. Tell him you will be placing the alarm clock on his side of the bed or buying him an alarm clock of his own—today. Tell him that, regardless of whether you are up or not, it will be his responsibility from now on to hear the alarm, wake himself up, get himself out of bed and make sure he is at work on time. No argument or discussion is needed. Before you go to sleep that night, you may want to remind him that the new "adult" routine starts in the morning. And leave it at that.

Be warned that the events of the following morning may be stressful for you but, having instigated a new routine, you *must* carry it through. If he turns his alarm off and promptly goes back to sleep, you must not make it your concern. You will feel tremendous pressure within yourself to revert to the mothering role, to go and wake him up so that he won't be late for work. Don't do it! If he is late for work, he is late for work. It's his own responsibility. Be prepared for some resistance and criticism at first, but don't give in. Be firm and, in particular, be firm with yourself. Instead of letting yourself slip back into old, unrewarding habits, set your sights on developing new and much more satisfying ones.

Expect your partner to be an adult (not a child)

Not only will your expectations of yourself change but you will also have different expectations of your partner. When you entered the relationship, you had certain expectations and now that you are maturing in your attitudes toward your own role, it is only to be expected that your expectations of your partner will change, too.

Men certainly have expectations when they begin a relationship. For many, it goes without saying that a woman will fulfil the traditional role and that the relationship will proceed according to the scenario of maternal woman and individual man. She will be there for him and he will be there for himself.

There are other men, I'm pleased to say, who enter long-term relationships with an expectation that they and their partner will have an equal relationship where responsibilities are shared. Sometimes the situation becomes confused by the fact that the woman does not have the same expectations. Later, when tensions are high in the relationship, a man will confide in a therapist or counsellor that he was "bowled over" by the fact that his partner insisted on doing everything for him. Many women are so eager to act according to their conditioning that, without thinking, they create a situation in the early months and years of their relationship that they later come to regret. The situation they create is one in which the woman is the efficient parent and the man is the helpless child.

While some men never feel comfortable with that kind of situation, most take very little time to adapt. They enjoy being pampered and adored and waited on, and why not? The parent–child roles then become entrenched and, before long, the woman begins to feel cheated of the adult–adult relationship she was looking for. Any attempts to effect changes, however, are met with resistance and resentment by a man who has come to expect to be mothered.

A woman who develops a determination to be an adult and not a parent to her partner, must have a firm expectation that her partner, also, will develop a determination to be an adult and not a child. The best way for a woman to begin, of course, is to sit down with her partner and talk to him about the changes she wants both of them to make. If, as is often the case with immature men, it is not possible to get your partner to engage in a serious discussion about the relationship, move on to the next step. The next step is: begin to relate to him as an adult (even while he is acting like a child). Stop doing all the "babying" things you used to do. Be prepared for some hurtful criticism, though. As mentioned in the introduction (p. 11), a man who feels he is losing some of his "privileges" can become very difficult. Remember, however, that this is his attempt to get his privileges back, to bring you back into the mothering role. If you stand firm, which you must do, then he will either become more determined and more entrenched in his man–child role or he will begin to move to a more adult way of relating. If he chooses the first option, then your hopes of an adult–adult relationship with him are dashed,* but if he chooses the second option, you can both look forward to a much more satisfying relationship.

---

* All you can do in this instance is maintain your determination to be an adult and not a parent. If there is no "parent" for a man–child to relate to, the child role is sometimes difficult to sustain, and change may still occur.

Boys will be boys

4. Trying to improve communication when you are the only one trying

Most women realise the value of communication. If two people in a relationship do not communicate in some meaningful way, that relationship will stagnate, and a stagnant relationship is a dead relationship. Most women know that. That's why so many of us put so much effort into keeping communication alive.

A closer look at the word "communicate" indicates that it is always a two-way process. Any word beginning with the prefix "com" usually refers to something two or more people do together. What that means is that if one person speaks and the other gives no response, communication has not taken place. All that has happened is that one person has spoken. Occasionally, I hear people incorrectly state that they have communicated *to* another person. The very meaning of the word makes it clear that communication is always done *with* another person or persons.

Put simply, communication consists of two activities: speaking and listening. When speaking, it is important to speak as clearly and concisely as possible, and when listening, it is important to listen as carefully and accurately as possible. But communication is not a simple matter. One of the complicating, but interesting, factors is that communication is nonverbal as well as verbal. Words are very important, but sometimes nonverbal communication is just as effective.* As a matter of fact, when there is an incongruence between verbal and

---

* Nonverbal communication includes facial expressions, tone of voice, degree of eye contact, body movements, bodily posture, sighing, yawning, silence.

nonverbal cues, it is often the nonverbal cue that rings more true. For example, when a man says "Of course I'm listening to you" but his eyes and ears are firmly fixed on the television, you can be pretty certain he isn't really listening. Or when a man has impatience and anger written all over his face, and yells "For God's sake, I do love you. What more do you want me to say?", you can be fairly certain that his nonverbals are closer to the truth at that moment than his words.

A concern expressed by some women is that there is no sign of communication coming from their partners at all. No words, no meaningful facial expressions, no eye contact. These women are given no clue at all as to what their partners are thinking or feeling (see Situation 6). It is not that their partners are *unable* to communicate, the women admit, because they see them interacting quite well with friends and workmates from time to time. For whatever reason, these men simply choose not to communicate with their wives and children.

Women living in such situations have attempted to compensate for the one-sided "communication" which consistently takes place in their relationship by developing a variety of responses. First, there is *the art of communicating for both of them*. A simple example:

Woman: How was work today?
Man: (Silence)
Woman: Pretty rough, eh? Sit down and I'll get
                   you a beer.

When a woman answers on behalf of her husband in this way, what she is actually doing is protecting herself from the devastation she would undoubtedly feel if she allowed herself to face up to the fact that he just didn't bother to respond to her question. He ignored her, treated her as if she didn't speak. For her own emotional protection, she sets up a situation where she can pretend they have communicated when, in actual fact, no communication took place at all. The truth is that because he chose not to respond, she has absolutely no idea how his day was. Her interpretation of his silence was that his day had been "pretty rough", but there are several other possible interpretations. He may have had a perfectly good day and been unhappy at having to leave work and come home. Or he may have been feeling desperately ill when he arrived home and didn't want to worry his wife. Or it may have been that he did not actually go to work and doesn't want his wife to know where he was. Or it could have been that he just couldn't be bothered answering, that he has such little respect for women in general, and his wife in particular, that he doesn't even consider the need to acknowledge that she has spoken.

This, of course, is what most women who develop the art of communicating for both of them are afraid of finding out. At some level, a woman may secretly suspect it to be true that her husband has no respect for women and, therefore, for her, but knows that if she goes on communicating for both of them, she may never have to find out.

Another common practice among women living with immature men is that they have developed *the art of reading into a man's behaviour meanings that are not there*. A woman says to herself, for example: "I know he still loves me. He just doesn't feel comfortable expressing emotion." Then, there is the all-too-common example of a woman putting a positive interpretation on her partner's behaviour by assuring their consistently disappointed children: "Your father doesn't mean to criticise you all the time. He really is proud of you. He just doesn't know how to show it."

A woman who interprets her partner's behaviour to mean something it clearly doesn't mean is, again, protecting herself from the pain of facing up to her fear. What if she is married to someone who just doesn't care, someone who has stopped loving her? She remembers times in the early months or years of their relationship when he did feel comfortable expressing emotions. Could he have lost the ability he once had? Or has he lost the love? There is a theory which says that immature men are good at communicating when they want something (or someone) but that once they get what they want, they don't bother any more. In other words, communication is something they do only when it will give them what they want.

Another practice some women engage in is *the art of leaving appropriate books lying around* in the hope that their partners will take the hint, pick the books up and read them. Men who have no interest in improving their communication skills will surely have no interest in reading books designed to help them improve their communication skills, but that does not seem to deter these women. They are ever hopeful that meaningful communication will one day be as important to their husbands as it is to them.

There is nothing wrong with leaving books around and nothing wrong with being hopeful so long as you also have a realistic understanding of your partner's level of interest. If you do, then you won't be too disappointed when he shows no interest and you'll be delighted when he does.

Suggestions for action

In your attempts to improve the communication in your relationship, it is necessary to remind yourself that the only behaviour you have the power to change is your own. If your partner does not want to change or improve his communication style, there is nothing you can do to make him change. That is why "trying to improve communication when you're the only one trying" is so frustrating. The following are a few things you *can* do.

Don't be too quick to blame yourself for the poor communication that exists in your relationship

Many women confess to being totally confused about the way some conversations proceed between themselves and their partners, and their immediate response is to blame themselves. But, in most instances, women are not to blame. A favourite pastime of some men is what I call *communication-sabotage,* and it occurs whenever the partner of one of those men initiates a serious conversation. Such a man deliberately sabotages every attempt she makes and she is left confused and frustrated. Even when a woman goes to great lengths to be clear and logical, such men will turn the conversation around so much that, before long, the original point is unrecognisable and the discussion goes nowhere. If you find yourself repeatedly confused and frustrated after attempts to communicate with your partner, be aware that the confusion created could be deliberate. Men who want to avoid serious conversations with their partners indulge in sabotage all the time. It is a clear example of immature men playing immature games.

Why is it that women are so quick to blame themselves for poor communication when, in fact, all the studies conclude unequivocally that women are much better communicators than men? It is probably because most of the criticisms we hear day after day, in the area of communication, are criticisms of women. We are told:

- women talk too much
- women gossip
- women talk nonsense
- women nag (harp)

- women are too emotional
- women aren't logical.

Several years ago, I read a book by Dale Spender* in which she described the findings of her research into this very issue. Women's communication is often criticised, she explained, because we live in a man's world and men act as if they own the language. In Dale Spender's terms, each of the above criticisms can be explained as follows.

Women talk too much

In a male-focused world where men's words, topics, opinions, judgements, pronouncements are the only forms of communication which seem to matter, women are expected to know their place and to keep silent. Women's role is to listen to men. Women *can* speak but only to facilitate men's speaking by asking questions and making encouraging remarks, thereby giving men the confidence to keep speaking. In work-related or social situations, if silence is the expectation for women, then any woman who seriously enters into a conversation, even just to say a few words, can be seen to be talking "too much". In the home, where men are much more silent, women's speech is still judged as "too much" because it interrupts the silence men insist on.

Women gossip

When women get together, the talk is much freer than when we are in mixed company. We enjoy talking and laughing together. Dale Spender's research showed that men often feel threatened by women-only talk. Hence, women's talk is often put down, and one of the favourite put-downs is to label it "gossip".

---

* Dale Spender (1980). *Man Made Language*. London: Routledge and Kegan Paul.

Women talk nonsense
Whenever a woman offers an opinion which is different from that of her husband, she is in danger of being accused of "talking nonsense". Her opinion may, in fact, be right but if it doesn't agree with her partner's opinion, it is "nonsense".

Women nag (harp)
Many women attest to the fact that when they say something and get no response from partner or children, they look for better ways of saying it. They presume they received no response because they didn't make their point clearly enough, so they try harder. Every time they are ignored, they keep trying harder. Women in these situations find themselves saying something over and over again. The result, of course, is that they are accused of nagging or harping. If such a situation were evaluated fairly, however, it would be said that because those to whom she was speaking chose to ignore her, she felt compelled to repeat herself over and over, in the hope that she would eventually receive a response.

Women are too emotional/not logical
Many women berate themselves for not being able to talk about something sad without being emotional, or for not being able to express anger without emotion. Sadness and anger *are* emotions and must be expressed emotionally. What could be more normal than crying when you are sad or expressing anger when you are angry? The expression of such emotions, however, makes many men feel uncomfortable and their response is to accuse their wives of being too emotional. "How can we have a logical conversation about this when you are so emotional?" Some men actually refuse to speak about an issue till their wives "pull themselves together" and "employ some logic". The sad thing is that many women

try very hard to do that and become impatient with themselves if they cannot stop their emotions engaging.

The way I see it is that if we suppress our emotions in an attempt to be coldly logical, we are letting ourselves down in the following ways.

- We are supporting men's belief that logic is much more important than emotion.
- We are betraying our own belief in the value and importance of emotions.
- We are giving in to men's demands that an issue can only be discussed or argued about if it is done on their terms.

Men feel comfortable with logic (even though many of them aren't very logical!). It follows, therefore, that any issue discussed at a logical level (that is, devoid of emotion), gives them a distinct advantage.

If we women are going to be true to ourselves and our belief in the value of emotion, we must make the point that logic and emotion belong together and that any conversation must allow room for both.

Be confident in your own ability to communicate

When we hear the above criticisms it is crucial that we refuse to accept them and that we go on believing in our own ability to be good communicators.

I said earlier that the two main areas of communication are speaking and listening. It would, actually, be more accurate to use the terms conveying a message and receiving a message. When one speaks, one is conveying a message, not just in words but also in nonverbal ways—mannerisms, attitudes, emotional content. When one listens, one is receiving and interpreting a message by taking notice of the nonverbal as well as the verbal content of that message.

In order to be good communicators, then, we must give attention to the following:
Speak (convey your message):
- clearly
- concisely
- confidently
- sensitively (that is, with emotion)
- logically

Listen (receive and interpret a message):
- carefully
- accurately
- confidently
- patiently
- sensitively

Have a realistic picture of the kind of communication that takes place in your relationship

How would you describe the communication in your relationship? However good or bad it might be, it is much better to have a realistic picture than to pretend it is something that it is not. If you are someone who has developed the art of communicating for both of you, then admit that to yourself. If you interpret your partner's silences to suit yourself instead of finding out what his silences really mean, if you have developed the art of reading into your partner's behaviour meanings that are not there, it is better to admit that rather than continue to fool yourself. Because fooling oneself is dishonest. When you put words into your partner's mouth so as to make it appear as if he is communicating, you may feel less anxious in the short-term, but be aware that it allows the rift between the two of you to grow wider and creates a situation where serious problems develop in the long-term. It is much better to find ways to insist on better communication. Make it clear that you refuse to live in a communication-vacuum. Observe him communicating with others and insist on, at least, that same level of communication at home.

Don't let your children get away with ignoring people

Good communication skills must be instilled in children from a young age. Boys are often allowed to get away with rudeness to adults and other children on the grounds that "boys will be boys". Most mothers accept behaviour from their sons that they would never accept from their daughters. Remember, if your husband is immature in the area of communication, your sons are learning from his bad example. If they get away with it, they will develop habits of communication which they will take with them into adult life.

If you teach your children that listening and responding to others is not just something they do after they have calculated "what's in it for me?" but, rather, that it is something they do because other people matter, then you will be going a long way toward helping them develop the kind of respect for others that will enable them to develop into sensitive and mature adults.

5. Longing for meaningful, stimulating conversation

When it comes to serious conversation, emotionally immature men seem to come in three varieties: those who have never involved themselves in meaningful conversation (and don't intend to start now); those who used to join in serious discussions but have long since left that behind; and those who do get involved in serious conversations but only if they can be the authority on every topic discussed.

Obviously, women who long for meaningful, stimulating conversation are not going to have that longing satisfied within their relationship when their partner belongs to one of the above categories.

"Never have and never will"

If you are married to a man in this first category, that is, those who never have and never will have a serious conversation, you must sometimes ask yourself how you came to be in that situation. But it's not difficult to see how it happens. In our society, there is still a lot of pressure on women to be married, and when a man comes along who clearly satisfies some of our needs, the majority of women seem to be prepared to take a risk. Also, some still make the mistake of believing that a man will change for the better after he is married, that all he needs is a little advice and help from his wife and he will become the kind of man she wants him to be. Even though this assumption has been proved wrong over and over again, the desire to be married is so strong that many women persist in their belief that it will be different for them.

There are two main types of "never have and never will" men:

- There are those who are always withdrawn and aloof, so aloof that they will never discuss anything with anyone. They come home from work and go straight to the computer or television. They rarely speak about anything, let alone anything meaningful.

- There are the jokers, those who love to tease, to ridicule, to make light of every situation that confronts them. In the beginning, a man like this appears to be fun-loving, the life of the party, and many women find such a man attractive. But when a woman tries to dig deeper, tries to get him to be serious, she often meets with strong resistance in the form of more "joking". It is then that she realises that the constant joking around is his way of avoiding any meaningful conversation.

Women in relationships with men who are either chronically aloof or chronically jovial, tend to spend an inordinate amount of time agonising over why he is like that. Why is he never interested in having a serious conversation? The explanations offered, while appearing to satisfy many women are, nevertheless, quite unsatisfactory in terms of the requirements of adult–adult relationships. The explanations (or excuses) women have come up with include: Some men just aren't capable of deep or intimate conversations. Or, some men are frightened of serious conversation because it challenges them and makes them feel vulnerable. Or, some men don't want to view themselves as "grown up". Having a serious, meaningful conversation would be a sign of maturity and they prefer to see themselves as young and rebellious and free.

I realise that women who want to continue in their relationships with immature men are desperate to find explanations for the absence of any attempt by their partner to participate in serious interactions. While I admit that looking for explanations is an important part of the process, it must be remembered that even when an "explanation" is found, the behaviour still persists. The distancing behaviour of "never have and never will" men continues and is a constant source of frustration for women who long for a relationship of substance.

"Used to"

The second category of men, that is, those who used to get involved in stimulating conversation but no longer do so, probably accounts for the majority of men whose partners are starved of meaningful, stimulating convers-ation.

Once the honeymoon period is over* and a relation-ship settles down into one of routine and predictability, communication can become dull and boring. The intimate and personal—"You're so lovely to be with"—turns into "Please pass the salt." The intellectually stimu-lating—"What do you think about China's one-child policy?"—turns into "Will you pick up the kids from basketball tonight?"

---

* The honeymoon period varies in length for different couples. It is inevitable that the passion, excitement and newness of a relationship will wear off, but there is no set time-frame. In relationships where there are no serious problems, the newness can last anywhere from six months to two years. On the other hand, some relationships lose their "special" quality after only a few weeks of a couple living together. Indeed, some women say they detected a definite change in the degree of interest shown by their partners almost as soon as their wedding vows had been said. On the wedding night itself, they noticed a distancing that hadn't been there before.

When that kind of situation develops, it is often because both partners are caught up in the rush and bustle of very busy lives. More often, though, the situation is that the woman makes time for conversation because she needs and wants to talk, but her husband does not. She remembers what it used to be like in the early months and years of their relationship, and misses that. She remembers how her partner used to enjoy sharing ideas about all kinds of interesting topics, and the intellectual stimulation was something that always brought them closer together. It is not uncommon for a woman to admit that the main attribute which attracted her to her husband in the first place was his ability to discuss issues and be excited by ideas and dreams and possibilities.

What happened to that idealistic, interesting, stimulating young man? Some theorise that adult men very quickly feel burdened by their perception of the weighty responsibilities that society places on their shoulders. As a consequence, the theory goes, they become narrowly focused on work and work-related matters, such as economics, ambition, competition, success (winning). Others theorise that adult men who feel reasonably satisfied with their lives see no reason to grow or change, and become almost totally focused on themselves. They see no reason to broaden their outlook beyond themselves. As a consequence, they narrow their interests down to those areas which immediately affect their own lives.

Whichever theory is true, the effect in terms of meaningful stimulating conversation is the same. A man who has narrowed his interests down to exclude anything that doesn't have an immediate bearing on himself, will have no interest in conversations that move beyond these bounds.

"Know-it-all"

The third category, that is, those men who enter into conversations for the purpose of showing how much they know, accounts for a substantial number of men in Western societies. Such men have no desire to be involved in the normal give and take of discussions between equals. They have no desire to learn from anyone else. As a matter of fact, they don't feel any *need* to learn anything, because they know it all. An acquaintance of mine described her situation like this:

> The talk that goes on between my husband and I could never be called a conversation. It's never a shared thing. He talks at me and, if I venture a point of view, he doesn't listen. He's only interested in making statements. And he's convinced he's always right.

It is true that such interactions cannot accurately be called conversations. A series of statements made by a self-professed authority, who has no interest in other people's responses, is more correctly called a monologue. Such boring, egotistical pontificating is a poor substitute indeed for meaningful, stimulating conversation.

Suggestions for action

Talk to your partner about what you need

If you are in a relationship that leaves you longing for substantial and meaningful interaction, the first thing you must do is talk to your partner about your needs in this regard. I realise you have probably tried to do that many times in the past, but do it one more time. Tell him you need more time where the two of you can talk together about serious things, about issues that interest you both. His response may be good but, given the fact that the raising of this issue on your part is actually an

women have spread themselves too thin with this juggling of marriage, career, and children

right as usual dear, marriage will have to go

Jacky Fleming (1992). *Never Give Up*. London: Penguin.

attempt at meaningful conversation, you should not be surprised if his response is negative. You could be accused of "going mad", of "making too many demands" on him, of being "selfish". Don't believe any of it. You could be met with stoney silence. You could be met with joking and ridicule. Or it could be the trigger that sends him straight to the TV or computer where he will bury himself till he thinks you're "over it". Nevertheless, it is worth a try.

If his attitude is negative, let your response be assertive

Whenever you make a reasonable request in your relationship and your request is ignored or met with ridicule or anger, it is crucial that you do not just passively accept the response and go about your life as if nothing has happened. Something *has* happened. As a matter of fact, something very serious has happened. You have made a reasonable request and your right to a reasonable response has been denied you. Remember, you are a worthwhile person and you have the right to expect that any request you make is taken seriously. You do not have the right to expect that all your requests will be *granted,* but you do have the right to expect to be taken seriously.

The very least you can do, then, in terms of making an assertive response, is express a desire to be taken seriously. Tell him that if he isn't interested in participating in meaningful conversation with you, he need only say so. There are other assertive responses you could make, of course, but this seems the most appropriate as an immediate response. Following that, you will have to decide if there are any other steps you want to take, based on how important it is to you that serious and meaningful conversation be part of your relationship.

Look elsewhere to satisfy your need for meaningful, stimulating conversation

Of course, it would be good to be able to share ideas and interests with the person you have chosen as your life's partner, but if that isn't happening or isn't likely to happen in the future, that doesn't have to spell the end of the relationship. Many women find intellectual stimulation and satisfaction with women friends, some with male friends, some by going to university, others by taking courses offered in the community. It is important not to neglect your need for meaningful interaction. My advice to you is, as I always tell myself, to open yourself up to opportunities as they present themselves.

6. When you never know what your partner thinks or feels

While the problems in relationships are many and varied, *imbalance in emotional satisfaction* is probably the most common, and emotional satisfaction is invariably connected with the degree to which one's partner is willing to share their thoughts and feelings. Generally speaking, men are satisfied with the emotional input and support they receive from their partners, while women feel emotionally deprived. In situations of relationship counselling, it is frequently the case that the man will say: "I don't know what she's complaining about. There's nothing wrong with our relationship apart from the fact that she keeps complaining." Most men seem to have no idea that the reason for their partner's dissatisfaction is that the woman is expected to go on giving day after day without receiving any emotional support in return, without as much as a hint about what her partner thinks or feels. This imbalance, and the negative effect it has on women, is borne out in the work of Shere Hite, American feminist and internationally renowned researcher and scientist, whose fifteen-year study provided valuable insights into the dynamics that exist between women and men.

One of the most interesting statistics in Hite's third report, *Women and Love*,* is that "98% of women say they would like their husband or lover to talk more about his feelings, thoughts, and dreams and to ask more about their own". In other words, almost all women feel

---

* Shere Hite (1987). *Women and Love. A Cultural Revolution in Progress*. London: Penguin, p. 806.

less than satisfied with the degree to which their partner is willing to share his intimate thoughts and feelings.

One of the questions in Hite's study was: "What is the biggest problem in your current relationship?" The following are some of the answers she received:

> His refusal to really share himself with me is a problem. I would like him to be more spontaneous, to talk deeply about his feelings, fears, or whatever. His ego doesn't permit it. I've yearned for sharing, but only get it with other friends. It could be better if he'd be more of a companion, talk more, have a sense of humor, and not consider his work so blastedly important.

> When I try to tell him my feelings or needs, he always says it's bullshit.

> I do more of the talking than he does. I would like more intimate talk, I wish he would tell me what he wants to happen in the future, but he doesn't talk to me. There seems to be a gap between us that grows as time goes on. Sometimes I feel like I can't share certain things with him because of what he might say or do. But I would love for both of us to share everything with each other. I don't know if that is possible or not.

> I would love to be able to really talk about everything— we have our moments but they're few and far between. I have to be very careful about what I say and how I say it. [pp. 5–7]

Today, more than ten years after the publication of Hite's research, it would appear that nothing much has changed. Women are still confiding in friends, therapists and marriage counsellors, desperate stories of the emotional neglect and loneliness they experience in their relationships with emotionally immature men.

Suggestions for action

If you are one of the 98 per cent of women whose relationship is not as emotionally satisfying as you would like, what can you do?

Talk to your partner about how you feel

The only action open to you, in the beginning, is to talk to your partner about your feelings of being shut out of his life and how important it is to you that he start sharing his thoughts and feelings with you. He may listen or he may not; he may care or he may not; but it is the only place for you to start.

Make time available for sharing thoughts and feelings

If both of you agree that you want a more balanced degree of emotional satisfaction in your relationship, you will begin by making time available so that it can happen. I still remember the simple words I read some years ago in a book dealing with the importance of setting goals and taking charge of one's own life: "If you want something to happen, make a space for it."* If both of you want more equal sharing, then both of you will begin by clearing away some of the clutter, the busyness, the excuses that exist in all of us individually, so that there is space for something new to happen.

It is a good idea to set aside half an hour or so every day (or every weekday) when top priority is given to sharing thoughts and feelings with each other. Make sure it is a real *sharing*, and doesn't deteriorate into a situation where one of you talks all the time and the other

---

* David Campbell (1974). *If you don't know where you're going, you'll probably end up somewhere else.* Allen, Texas: Argus Communications, p. 113.

listens all the time. There will be times, of course, when what you share is silence. Talking is important, but it is not always necessary or helpful that every moment you spend together be filled with words.

When to set aside the time will depend on whether or not you have children and, if so, the ages of your children. Some couples enjoy sitting down together after work, having a drink, and talking about the events and emotions of the day before beginning to cook dinner. Couples with children, on the other hand, find it impossible to talk about anything of substance at that time of the day. Some prefer early in the morning or late at night. Providing children are not too young to be left alone in the mornings, a good habit to develop is that of getting up early and going for a walk together before the day begins. Walking and talking in the early morning is a good way to start the day and, as a bonus, the exercise does wonders for your physical and emotional health.

In the event that your partner is not interested in working at developing a more balanced degree of emotional satisfaction in your relationship, then I doubt the above strategies will work, but they may still be worth a try. Who knows what might happen? If he agrees to go walking with you every morning for the exercise only, he may one day just start talking as well!

7. When you are the butt of his "jokes"

Something I value highly in relatives and friends is a sense of humour. I like good-natured humour, that is, humour that does not depend for its laughs on putting someone else down. Much of what passes for humour these days boils down to enjoyment at the expense of others, and I don't like that. I don't want to laugh when other people are hurt.

As contradictory as it may sound, though, I do like good satire, which is actually dependent for its laughs on making fun of the pretensions and actions of powerful people and institutions. I enjoy humour that is clever, and good satire which uses humour to raise people's awareness of hypocrisy, greed and corruption wherever they are found, is clever. The targets of satire are usually politicians, business leaders, union leaders, professionals, the media, and while satirical humour is not meant to be good-natured it, nevertheless, serves a good end. It serves to remind powerful people and institutions that they are under scrutiny and that they are expected to exercise care and responsibility in all their dealings.

What about humour in relationships? Is there any humour in your relationship and, if so, what kind of humour is it? The kind that works *for* a relationship and not *against* it, is that which is shared and enjoyed by both partners. Sadly, what often passes for humour is a situation in which one partner is always being "funny" and the other is always being hurt.

I'm reminded, here, of a radio program a year or so ago in which a man was being interviewed about his friend who had just died. His friend had been a celebrity in his field of expertise and well-known in the community. As the interview progressed, I became quite interested in the story of this man's life. But then the interview turned to what the person being interviewed called his friend's "wonderful sense of humour". To illustrate it, he told a story about how this man's wife had pleaded with him for a couple of years to fix the letterbox which was so broken down that the mail would slide out of it and fall on to the ground. When he didn't look like fixing it, she said she would get a handyman in and pay him to fix it. No, her husband wouldn't hear of that. (Sounds familiar, doesn't it?) So the letterbox remained in its broken-down state. One day, after his wife spoke to him about it yet again, this "funny" man took a hammer and saw and went down to the old letterbox, knocked it down, and replaced it with a plastic bucket.

The man telling the story was laughing too much to continue speaking. He was so amused by this "hilarious" incident that he had to stop and compose himself before the interview could proceed. I myself was not amused. What I saw was a cruel act by an arrogant and self-centred man. And a woman who was treated badly by his shabby behaviour. Not only were her pleas ignored but, also, she was made the butt of his cruel joke. I imagine her distress at this put-down, her frustration and her terrible isolation as she watched all his mates, in the ensuing weeks, laughing and slapping him on the back. What a good joke! And what a clever joker!

Dale Spender's introduction to Judy Horacek's book of cartoons, *Life on the Edge*, is very enlightening.* She

---

* While my comments here focus only on the Introduction, I highly recommend Judy Horacek's cartoons. Sending up everyday situations from a woman's perspective, they are clever, funny, subversive—and most enjoyable. See Judy Horacek (1992/2003). *Life on the Edge*. Melbourne: Spinifex. The quotations that follow are from pp. v–viii.

talks about humour and its relationship to power. Since men are the ones with power in our society, she says, "it is no accident that it has been men who have enjoyed the right to be humour makers. Nor is it an accident that women have been defined as the individuals who have no sense of humour, and whose role it is to serve as the butt of the joke."

In many of the relationships I have observed, it is exactly as Dale Spender says: the man is the joker, the woman is the butt of his jokes and, when she complains about being ridiculed and humiliated, she is told she has no sense of humour. Because men own the right to be "funny", women know they must always be prepared for the likelihood that they will be the butt of male humour. In mixed company, at a barbecue or a dinner party, for example, the message to women is clear: "Learn to put up with the 'jokes', with the teasing, or risk being label-led a prude, a plaintive guest, or a 'party pooper' with no sense of humour." In other words, "when men want to be funny, then women had better learn to laugh, or to take the consequences". Most women know what our role is in relation to male humour. We know we are required to give undivided attention while the joke is being told and then, when the time is right, to laugh, even when the "joke" is unfunny or hurtful.

The comparison Spender makes between male and female humour helps us understand why women find so much of men's humour unfunny, and why women have so little interest in participating "in the customary joke-making of society".

There can be no doubt that men have declared the traditional forms of humour to be a boys' game and have determined to keep women out. But neither can there be any doubt that most women have not been impressed by the game, and have decided that they do not want to play.

This is partly because it has been common practice for the joke teller, the humourist, to "seize the floor", to monopolise attention, claim space, and insist on his own view of the world and his own right to speak; and none of these characteristics sits comfortably with women's customary conversation codes.

While men's humour is often aggressive and controlling, women's humour usually reflects an emphasis on cooperation and community. When women are funny, we are funny together. Humour is something we share. It is a strategy we use "for promoting common understandings among women—and for promoting change".

Continuing the comparison, those who have studied humour point out that much of men's humour makes use of a victim, a scapegoat, someone who is "the butt of the joke". Women's humour, on the other hand, may mock, expose, satirise, but "rarely are there any *scapegoats* in women's humorous anecdotes and exchanges". Most women don't want to participate in the kind of humour that laughs at the misfortunes of others, nor do we want to pretend to enjoy it when we, ourselves, are made the butt of men's jokes.

Suggestions for action

Explain to your partner (again) that it hurts and embarrasses you when he makes you the butt of his "humour"

I wish I could assure you that your partner will stop making jokes at your expense once you have explained to him how it makes you feel, but the experience of women over the years is that men who are "jokers" don't change their behaviour easily. They certainly don't change as a result of their partner's pleading with them or explaining how hurt and embarrassed she feels. That doesn't seem to matter. What does matter, it seems, is whether or not the joker gets a response. If a woman makes a determined effort to steel herself against his put-downs, to make absolutely no response, no laughing, no crying; if she carries on interacting with her guests; and if the guests take their cue from her and also give no response, he will soon find no enjoyment in it. There's not much point in continuing to be a joker if no one is laughing. He will stop, not because it is hurting you, but because "you have no sense of humour".

Your first move must be to explain how you feel. If your feelings are important to him, he will stop. But if his own need for power and attention are all that matter to him, then he will continue being the joker regardless of how it makes you feel.

Don't laugh just because it is expected of you

Whether it is your partner or someone else who is the joker, don't feel you have to laugh at anyone's attempts at humour just because women are expected to feign amusement. If you are not amused, then don't pretend you are. If you think a person's humour is cruel, say so—and ask them to stop.

Get in touch with your own sense of humour and enjoy it

Women and men who are interested in and care about others have the potential for a rich and extremely funny sense of humour. It comes, I believe, from the ability to watch people, to observe their interactions and to allow oneself to see the funny side of things. Women, in particular, are often very good at analysing situations and sensing what's going on at many different levels.

While women do have the potential for a good sense of humour, many admit that the pressures and demands of life seem to have caused them to lose their ability to laugh.

Work at getting back your sense of humour—and enjoy it. Many things in life are funny. The idea of men strutting around making out that they are so superior is funny. Women pretending to be inferior so as not to upset men's fragile egos can be funny. Politicians trying to convince themselves and us that they are so important and that they are actually worth all the money they pay themselves can be funny. Your children and the things they say and do at times can be funny.

Analyse your own sense of humour so that you are aware of the kinds of situations and jokes you find amusing. And look for other people who share your kind of humour. Laughter is still the best medicine and sharing good, wholesome humour with others is great for one's sense of well-being.

8. When you are made to feel invisible

Do you ever have times when you want to call out: "Hello. Am I here? Will someone please tell me if they can see me?" You just feel invisible. You speak and nobody turns a head. Nobody responds with even a flinch. It is as if you didn't speak, but you know you did.

It happens to women in all kinds of situations. In the home, it is common for women's remarks or questions to be ignored totally by husbands and children. They all just keep doing what they are doing and feel no compulsion even to acknowledge that someone has spoken. At the workplace, women often have the experience of being ignored. It is not simply that our opinions and suggestions are rejected after having been heard and considered, but that we are totally ignored, not listened to. When this happens to me, I experience a momentary feeling of unreality that can be quite distressing. After I take time to remind myself of what has happened, that is, that I have been rendered invisible by someone (or a group of people) whose attitude toward women is that we are not worth listening to, my feeling of unreality turns to annoyance or anger and then I feel better.

Recently, I contacted my computer suppliers about having more bytes installed in my computer. A young man was subsequently sent out to my office to do the installation—a pleasant, well-mannered young man. As he proceeded with what turned out to be a fairly simple task, I took the opportunity to seek his opinion about what might have caused the large stain which had begun to appear on the top of my computer soon after I bought it, and which has grown darker and more obvious ever since. He said: "Looks like somebody spilled a cup of coffee on it", to which I replied politely: "No, that's not it. I work alone here and I'm the only one who has access

to my computer. I've never had coffee anywhere near it."
The young man gave no response to what I had said but
continued with the task of installing the bytes. Then,
after a minute or two of total silence, he said: "Yeah,
that's what it would be. Someone's spilt coffee on it."

Did I speak, I wonder? Or was I just imagining that
I said nobody could have spilled coffee on my computer
because I'm the only one who has access to it? Being
rendered invisible is a very strange and unsettling feeling
but it is one that women have to contend with almost
every day.

Women tell of experiences in social situations, too,
where they wish they could actually disappear because
being made to feel invisible while still being visible is
nothing short of humiliating. Accompanying one's husband or partner to a social evening with his work col-
leagues can be a particularly devastating experience. It
is not uncommon for a woman, on arrival, to be totally
ignored by the host who makes a fuss of her husband,
introducing him all around while she trails along behind
as a mute and invisible appendage. She could bear the
host's rudeness if only her partner could be depended
upon to have enough sensitivity to see what is happening
and ensure that she is included, but that is so often not
the case. Men in these situations seem to get caught up
with the importance of being the centre of attention and
their delight at being fussed over only adds to the
woman's feelings of invisibility. The worst part for a
woman is when her partner leaves her alone to fend
for herself while he goes off to circulate. She observes
him across the room, chatting, drinking, laughing and
generally enjoying himself with everyone else while she,
in contrast, spends the evening attempting to make conversation with strangers, many of whom look at her as if
to say: "Who are you?"

There are, also, those social occasions with friends when the men dominate the conversation. Most of the discussion on such occasions focuses on topics of interest mainly to men and, when women attempt to join in the conversation, they often find themselves being ignored, talked over or interrupted. When a woman speaks, it is not unusual for the subsequent conversation to proceed as if she had not spoken. For example, a man in the group (Marco) gives his opinion about an issue and that is followed by the opinion of a woman (Lucia). Then, a third person in the group speaks up and says: "I don't know if I agree with you, Marco . . . etc.". The conversation proceeds as if Lucia had not spoken and Lucia is left to wonder how her contribution could have been so uninteresting as to be so totally ignored. Women are made to feel invisible in many ways and on many occasions.

Suggestions for action

The one thing women should not do when rendered invisible by others is accept it. What we normally do when someone has ignored us is keep our distress hidden and tell ourselves we are just being silly. We work hard at convincing ourselves that it would be petty to complain. We tell ourselves it isn't important when, in fact, the opposite is true.

Being made to feel invisible is not a trivial matter. It represents an assault on the core of one's being and, as such, has the potential for causing serious emotional and psychological damage. Anxiety problems, panic attacks and agoraphobia often have their beginnings in persistent experiences of being made to feel invisible.* Depression, also, is a common result of the experience of invisibility.

---

* See chapter four of my book, *Overcoming Anxiety: A positive approach to dealing with severe anxiety in your life* (1992). Sydney: Allen & Unwin.

Change the way you think when you are rendered invisible

Instead of turning your attention in on yourself and asking: "What's wrong with me?" turn your attention outwards and ask: "What's wrong with them?" Instead of punishing yourself with thoughts that you are "boring" or "not worth listening to", allow yourself to look outside yourself and analyse the behaviour of the other person or persons. If you can label the behaviour of the one who rendered you invisible as "downright rude" or "self-absorbed" or "arrogant", then you will avoid personal feelings of emptiness and nothingness and, instead, experience the much more healthy feelings of indignation and anger.

Turn invisibility into visibility

Because invisibility can have such harmful effects, it is crucial to a woman's emotional health that she refuse to be ignored. Remember that nobody can render you invisible if you refuse to be invisible, so spend some time developing ways to make your presence felt. The following are some suggestions.

When what you say is totally ignored, say something like: "I'll keep on saying this till someone answers me."

On those occasions when you are interrupted in mid-sentence, you can do one of two things. You can interrupt the person right back and say "Let me finish what I'm saying" or "I want to finish what I'm saying", and then proceed. Don't wait for anyone's approval to proceed. Act as if it is your right to finish what you started out to say—because it is. Your other option is to wait till the person finishes and then say "As I was saying . . .". Or, if you want to make the point more strongly: "As I was saying before I was interrupted . . .".

Jacky Fleming (1992). *Never Give Up*. London: Penguin.

In those social situations where your partner is introduced and your presence is barely acknowledged, take a step forward, smile broadly and confidently, offer your hand as if expecting a handshake, and say: "And I'm Mandy Lau. I'm pleased to meet you."

I realise these confrontational kinds of responses do not come easily to most women but, in the interests of our own emotional health and happiness, we need to stop passively accepting whatever happens to us and develop the ability to be more assertive. Practise the assertive responses mentioned above so that, next time someone attempts to render you invisible, you will be ready to respond in a way that reclaims your visibility.

Over the years, women have tried practical ways, too, of discouraging invisibility and promoting their visibility. Some make very good use of straw hats for every occasion; some become known for their scarves or for their "different" hairstyles and colours. If there is something practical that appeals to you and you decide to try it, be sure to do it with flair and confidence, and you will be noticed!

Be careful not to render other women invisible

Men are not the only ones who ignore or interrupt women and treat them as if they are not there. Sometimes women, in their attempts to be more assertive and visible, find themselves doing to other women what is so often done to them. In our enthusiasm to jump into a conversation and be heard, it is easy to forget and inadvertently interrupt or talk over other women. In practising our new assertiveness, then, let's be sure to maintain our sensitivity to the needs and rights of others.

9. When you are always the one who is wrong

If you live with a man who is always "right", I'm sure you have asked yourself many times: How can one person be right 100 per cent of the time and another be wrong 100 per cent of the time? Well, of course, they can't. It defies logic. But then, immature and self-absorbed men are not often logical! When the world begins and ends with oneself, it is not possible to have a balanced view of the world and its interactions.

I still have a memory of a time in my life when I always thought I was right. I guess most people experience a period like that in their teenage years, but hardly remember it because it is a normal and natural part of growing up. The reason I can still remember that part of my growing up is probably because, when it finally occurred to me that I was perhaps *not* always right, the realisation was quite profound. As a young teenager, I was not loudly and arrogantly right. Quite the contrary, I was serious and thoughtful and intense and religious— and right! I *knew* I had all the right answers (after all, I had God on my side!) and I sincerely wanted others to be convinced by my well-thought-out opinions and arguments.

It wasn't until I started studying at around eighteen or nineteen and began to mature intellectually and emotionally, that I realised I did not have all the answers and I was not always right. Maturity allows us to see that, even though we may be totally convinced by our own perceptions and opinions, other people also are totally convinced by *their* perceptions and opinions. And when their opinions differ from ours, it can never be a simple matter of "I'm right and you're wrong." We are both right, according to our individual perceptions. That is why mature people value the art of negotiation and compromise. First, there is a willingness to listen and a genuine desire to understand where the other person is coming from. Then, in those situations where agreement is essential, there is a willingness to compromise, to give a little, to negotiate a position which is acceptable to both.

Sometimes, when a compromise is not possible, when a satisfactory mutual position cannot be found, it is necessary to agree to differ. Mature people respect each other's right to hold differing opinions and, indeed, respect the opinions of others, without necessarily agreeing with them.

Suggestions for action

If you are in a relationship with a man who always has to make you wrong so that he can go on deluding himself that he is always right (and if you don't want to leave him to stew in his arrogant "rightness" all alone!), there are certain things you must do.

Stop trying to figure it out

As mentioned earlier, many women spend hours and days and years of their lives trying to figure out why their husbands behave the way they do. Such a woman believes that, if only she could figure out what causes her partner to think he is always right, she could explain it to him, he would be grateful for the explanation, and he would change. But it isn't a simple matter of lack of understanding. Rather, it is a matter of lack of desire. He has no *desire* to understand. He doesn't *want* to stop and analyse his behaviour. He doesn't *want* an explanation. Because he doesn't *want* to change. He likes being "right". And if his being right means he has to make everyone else wrong, so be it.

So, you see, there is no need to spend your life trying to figure out why your partner always has to "prove" you wrong, because there is nothing to figure out. The explanation is simply that he hasn't matured beyond a childish obsession with himself as the centre of the universe. And until he does, there will be no change in his behaviour.

Don't waste your energy arguing with someone who is always right

Immature men seem to think it is a sign of weakness to admit they have made a mistake, while the rest of us know that making mistakes and being wrong occasionally is a normal part of life. Indeed, to be able to admit to having made a mistake is a sign of strength and maturity.

When an immature man is guarding against what he perceives to be weakness, any attempt to argue or reason with him will be fruitless. Similarly, any attempt to explain to him that it is not weak to admit to being wrong, will also be fruitless. It is never possible to get through to someone whose mind is firmly closed.

Have you ever wondered why women persist in arguing or trying to reason with someone like that? I think it has something to do with justice. Many women say to me: "But it's just not right. There's no justice in it. He shouldn't be allowed to go on thinking he's always right." I agree. But the fact is, an immature man *will* continue to think he's right no matter how much energy you use up trying to convince him to see things differently. So don't waste your energy. It is far better for you to disengage from any argument which has a predetermined result. In other words, avoid any argument or discussion with any person who begins with the supposition that you are wrong, and try to content yourself with the knowledge that your opinion was formed through careful thought and intelligent reasoning.

Trust your own intelligence

One of the unfortunate side-effects in women living with men who are always "right", can be the development of chronic self-doubt. If a woman is told often enough that she is wrong, that she doesn't know what she is talking about, it is easy to see how she would begin to believe it. One woman summed up her experience after eighteen years of marriage by saying:

> As a young woman, I was bright, intelligent, confident, articulate. Now, after being married to an arrogant know-all for eighteen years, I feel like a blithering idiot. Scared to speak for fear of making a fool of myself. Absolutely no confidence in my ability to string two words together and have them make sense.

If you are living in this kind of situation, it is crucial you take account of how badly you are being affected by the constant assault on your intelligence. If you decide to stay in the relationship, it is imperative that you develop the ability to close off to your partner's insults and open yourself up to the opinions of people who are not afraid to respect and affirm your intelligence. Your ability to trust and respect your own intelligence will be strengthened as you associate with others who trust and respect your intelligence.

10. When you sense you are being lied to

Dishonesty, in terms of not telling the truth, can take the form of telling outright lies or of withholding the truth in an attempt to deceive. Both forms of dishonesty are common in relationships in Western cultures. A closer look at the matter of dishonesty in relationships reveals that, while both sexes can be said to be equally dishonest, the issues around which women and men lie or attempt to cover up the truth and deceive each other are generally not the same.

The one issue which does seem to generate the same degree of dishonesty from both sexes is the issue of extra-marital affairs. In such situations, women and men go to equally elaborate lengths to cover up evidence of their unfaithfulness. They seem to be content to live the lie day after day, and somehow manage to convince themselves that their spouse is better served by not knowing than knowing.*

Apart from the situation of unfaithfulness, the issues around which women are dishonest are quite different from those associated with men's dishonesty. The two main issues around which women tend to lie or deceive their partners are: money spent on day-to-day living, and problems associated with the children. When women do lie about money, it is usually about comparatively small amounts spent on particular items. For example, it is fairly common for a woman to buy an article of clothing (dress, swimsuit, shoes) for herself or one of the children, and tell her husband it cost considerably less than it did,

---

* For a more detailed discussion of the effects of suspecting one's partner is having an affair, see Situation 25.

or actually hide it till she figures out how to "confess" to him.*

A woman's decision to lie to her partner about the behaviour of their children is an interesting one, too. It is usually done in collusion with the children, and most often takes the form of withholding information. If a child's behaviour at school has been such that the mother has been contacted by the teacher or school principal, the mother will often make a pact with the child to hide the truth from the father on the condition that the child's behaviour improves. Similarly, when a child has committed a crime, like shoplifting, and is cautioned by police, mothers often ask the police not to involve the father. Although such withholding of information about children's behaviour is sometimes rationalised as "not wanting to worry their father", it is often done out of fear that the father's punishment will be excessive or inappropriate.

Men's dishonesty in relationships is different from that of women in that it often relates to larger issues. When a man withholds information about money, for example, it is often about large amounts of money. Some men will commit themselves to buying a boat or a car or a block of land, and withhold the information from their wives till it is too late to cancel the contract. Others lose large amounts of money through gambling and, in some

---

* This kind of withholding of information occurs with some women even when they live with partners who are not at all concerned about how much money their wives spend. In some instances, the women are simply imitating the behaviour they remember their mothers engaged in. In other instances, women do it out of their own sense of guilt. They feel they have no right to spend money on themselves and, when they do, they must hide it in an attempt to avoid "punishment".

instances, cover up the fact that loan repayments and other essential bills have not been paid for months.

Telling lies or withholding information involving large amounts of money usually has grave consequences for both partners. When a man spends beyond his means or gambles away his money, he is generally using money that belongs to both partners jointly, and the financial debt incurred will be a burden on both of them for years into the future.

Another area of dishonesty for some men concerns the use of pornographic magazines and videos. Most women who discover pornography in their homes admit to feeling disgusted and betrayed. When they confront their partners they are most often met with promises that it will never happen again, but women in these situations are never really sure. They would like to be able to trust their partners' word, but find themselves wondering if the lies, the betrayal, the exploitation of women are continuing underground.

Suggestions for action

When you sense you are being lied to, but are not sure, make it your business to find out. Not knowing is much worse for you than knowing. The first and easiest step is:

Discuss your suspicions with your partner

I realise it may sound naïve to suggest you talk with your partner about your suspicions, because if he has set his mind on deceiving you, there is no way a simple question from you will reverse his intentions. If you tell him about your uneasy feelings and ask him if he is lying to you, you can be almost certain he will deny it. But, for many women, this is an important first step.

If you do decide to talk to your partner about your suspicions, be prepared for anything. A man who is put on the spot and feels the need to defend his lies usually does so vigorously. He may ignore you, sidestep your question, change the subject, sulk. He may turn on the charm so that you end up feeling guilty that you ever thought him capable of deceiving you. He may become very angry, insult you, call you "mad" or "paranoid" or "ungrateful".

If, after surviving his reaction, you still sense you are being lied to, make up your mind to do some investigating.

Look for proof

When your instincts tell you your partner is actively lying to you or passively withholding the truth from you, trust your instincts and pursue it further. When your attempts to discuss your suspicions with him fail, begin to look for proof. You may not actually *want* to know because you sense the truth would be painful for you but, psychologically, it is far better for your emotional health if you know. Once you know the truth, it's out in the open and is much easier to deal with. Suspecting but not knowing causes depression and/or anxiety. Suspecting but not knowing places you in a position of living every day with something unknown hanging over you, haunting you, causing you to feel fear and dread. There is nothing worse than living in fear of something that has no name, no shape, no identity. But, of course, deciding to look for proof is never easy.

Women who have been deceived about financial matters, for example, will admit, after the fact, that even though they had a feeling for many months that the bills were not being paid, they could not bring themselves to phone the bank or the agent. The thought of checking up on their husband seemed so disloyal. It wasn't until the telephone or electricity was about to be cut off that they finally had to confront their suspicions and deal with the consequences of not acting sooner. Others who suspect their partner is having an affair or using pornography admit that they, too, are reluctant to look for proof. They want to believe it isn't true. They try to convince themselves they are just being "paranoid". They don't want to know and yet, at the same time, they feel they have to know. It is never easy.

If you suspect your partner is lying to you and your suspicions are persistent, do look for proof. The sooner you know the truth, the sooner you can begin to do something about it. In the event that you find no proof, your fears will most probably settle down. If they don't, it goes without saying that you are faced with a difficult decision. The best thing to do, if you can, is to proceed as if your partner is telling the truth. Make up your mind that you will believe him until such time as proof of your suspicions surfaces because, without confirmation of your suspicions, you have no basis on which to negotiate a change in your partner's behaviour. If you are unable to put your fears aside, however, you are left with no other option but to finish the relationship in an attempt to release yourself from the mental agony you are experiencing.

Confront the lies—and the liar

If you do find proof, you are then in a position to consider your options. The first thing you will notice is that there has been a definite change in your feelings. The bad feelings you have been experiencing for some time will leave you, but they will be replaced by another set of bad feelings. Usually, a woman who finds proof to support her suspicions changes from feeling powerlessness and fear and dread, to betrayal and embarrassment and anger. While the second group of feelings is no easier than the first, they are far less damaging to one's psychological health. Once you discover the truth, you are one step closer to resolving the question of what to do about your relationship.

One option is to pack up and leave. If his betrayal has filled you with sufficient anger and you see no hope for a satisfactory reconciliation, then you will choose this option. The talking, the arguing, the expression of emotions which need to occur in order that you can let go of the relationship and move on, can happen later.

Another option, once you have found proof, is to do absolutely nothing. Accept that he is a gambler and will gamble away all your money till you live in abject poverty, or accept that he is having an affair or exploiting women and children through pornography, and try to organise your relationship around his dishonesty and deceit. Some women pride themselves on "knowing but not letting on they know", on living as if the betrayal were not true. This option, this unacknowledged collusion with one's partner's lies, is *not* recommended.

A third option is the one most women choose. On finding proof of their partners' lies, they confront. Women generally believe that if two people love each other and one is caught out in a lie or an act of betrayal, a confrontation and a discussion will be followed by an apology and then reconciliation is possible. A word of advice: your task, in such a situation, is to find a way to resolve your own feelings about what has happened. It is important that your resolution of the matter not depend on your partner's agreeing with you or apologising for his behaviour. The experience of many women is that a genuine admission and a genuine apology rarely come.

The usual ways immature men respond to being found out are either to turn the whole thing around and find a way to blame their partners, or to con their partners with a show of remorse (often with tears and apologies and promises), only to revert to their old ways within weeks.

Regardless of the way your partner responds to your confrontation, important priorities for you must be your own emotional survival and your own right to make decisions about your future.

11. Always waiting for the "right" moment to talk to him

When I first became a counsellor, I was amazed at the number of women who would tell me that I was the first person who had listened to them for a long time. Throughout the years, it has been confirmed for me over and over again that, when women want and need to talk about something, the people closest to them often don't want to listen.

Different women respond to this in different ways. Some rarely speak unless they are spoken to. Some talk non-stop as a way of compensating. Some express their true thoughts and feelings only when they are in the company of women. Some only relax and feel comfortable when they are looking after children.

Others, perhaps the majority of women, still persist in their attempts to speak with their husbands, and because it is so important to them, many are prepared to wait for the "right" moment to do it. In one sense, such women are to be congratulated for their initiative in developing ways whereby they will not be crushed by their partner's lack of interest and lack of involvement. In another sense, it is deeply sad that so many women have to "duck and weave" in this way. Communication ought to be a simple matter of one person speaking and the other listening and responding. On those occasions when one person speaks and the other doesn't feel ready to listen or to discuss an issue, it ought to be a simple matter of the second person saying "I'm not ready to talk about this yet", or "I need time to think about this. Let's talk about it tomorrow morning."

Good communication is uncomplicated and fair to both parties. But when a woman has to watch and wait for those times when she thinks her partner may be open to hearing her speak, when she has to take a deep breath and risk his wrath if she has chosen the wrong time, communication is turned into a nightmare.

It is not uncommon for a woman to spend hours, or even days, preparing herself for a conversation with her partner. Anxious to avoid a repeat of past experiences when he stubbornly refused to listen, repeatedly cut her off in mid-sentence, exploded in anger, or belittled her in cruel and mocking tones, she plots and plans and prepares.

Having prepared what to say and how to say it, she then waits. Good timing is everything. If she speaks when he is not ready to listen, all her preparation will have been for nothing. So she waits and watches, always in tune with his moods, always alert to his signals, always at the ready. She knows, too, that when the "right" moment arrives, she will have to strike swiftly, before the opportunity is lost.

Also, she knows she will have to be concise. Most women have learned the art of rationing their words. Experience has taught us that if we do not speak in as few words as possible, we will be interrupted, talked over, cut off, pushed aside.

So, the stage is set. You are ready. All you have to do is wait for the right moment. It is your hope, as always, that a moment will come when your partner will *want* to hear what you have to say, but you know from past experience that the best you can expect is that a moment will emerge when your partner is less resistant, more receptive.

If you are one of those women who find themselves waiting for the "right" moment to talk to their partners about something they know their partners won't want to hear, be aware of how much of your time and nervous energy you are devoting to a lost cause. Think about how much of your life is spent waiting, watching, anticipating, rehearsing your words, living on the edge of your nerves, and ask yourself if that is really how you want to live the rest of your life.

Suggestions for action

Be spontaneous and confident, regardless of his mood

If you want good, effective, adult communication in your relationship, have the courage to be spontaneous. The ability and willingness to be spontaneous is essential if your communication style is to reflect maturity. To hesitate, to wait, to attempt to manipulate, is not an example of adult communication. It is important that you relate to your partner as if he were capable of adult responses. In other words, when you have something you need to talk to him about, just do it. Don't agonise over it. Don't wait for the right moment. Don't dance around his moods.*

Speak confidently. Speak as if you have the right to say what is on your mind. Because you do.

In terms of psychological health, remember this: *It is far better to deal with the consequences of speaking spontaneously than to waste nervous energy waiting for a moment that may never come.* Another consideration is that if you relate to your partner in an adult way, it gives him the opportunity to respond in an adult way. You never know, he may surprise you!

---

* An emphasis on spontaneity, of course, does not mean you will suspend common sense. For example, to raise a serious issue with your partner just as guests are about to arrive for dinner would defeat your purpose. Choose a quiet time and go for it.

Don't blame yourself

When a woman waits for the "right" moment to raise an issue with her partner and it doesn't work out as she had hoped, her immediate reaction is to blame herself for "getting it wrong". But it is not usually her fault. I cannot emphasise this strongly enough. When you are in such a situation, that is, when you wait for the right moment and it doesn't work out, remember that it is most probably not your fault. If a man doesn't want to talk about an issue, no moment will be the right moment. Whatever moment you choose, it will always be the "wrong" moment.

So, stop blaming yourself. It is not that you didn't judge the timing accurately, or that you said too much or too little, or that you may have sounded accusing when you meant to sound understanding and compassionate. It is simply that he didn't want to hear what you were saying. In such situations, men often heap blame on their partners as a way of defending themselves ("You're always harping." "You're always dragging up the past." "Just when we seem to be getting along well, you spoil it by talking about something that annoys me."). Whatever you do, don't accept the blame.

Regardless of how your partner may respond, the rules of good communication, together with the requirements of your mental health, demand that you say what is on your mind. I am not saying you have the right to speak ruthlessly and destructively, but you do have the right to say what is on your mind and to say it spontaneously and confidently. All that is left, then, is for you to be prepared to deal with consequences.

12. When you are constantly told you are mad (and half believe it)

Believe me when I say that if your partner and his supporters are the only ones saying you are mad, you most
probably are not. The easiest way to find out is to ask
one of your friends to give you feedback about the way
they perceive you to be—your thought-patterns, the way
you speak, the way you behave.

During my years as a psychotherapist, I have seen
many women who have come to talk to me for the
express purpose of having me give my verdict on whether
or not they were "mad". Not one of these women was
insane, but all the years of listening to their partners
telling them they were mad had worn them down so
much that they were losing the ability to believe in their
own sanity.

Any woman living with an immature man needs to
remember that the accusation "mad" usually means:
"You're disagreeing with me and I don't like it." Or
"How dare you question my authority." Or "I'm so
insecure within myself that the only way I can feel good
about myself is to insult and hurt someone else."

It makes you wonder, doesn't it, who the "mad" one
really is?

13. When you feel you have to keep your anger to yourself

Anger that is kept inside is bad for you. Most people imagine that if they can control their anger, it will just go away. But it doesn't. It stays locked up inside and churns around looking for a way out. The power of anger is such that, if it is deprived of its normal way out, that is, through normal expression, it will find its own way out. Depression, for example, is often the expression of unexpressed anger. Bitterness, sarcasm, irritability, pettiness are also expressions of unexpressed anger.

Women who keep their anger to themselves often find themselves standing helplessly by, watching their own personalities change. They have no idea as to why they have become depressed or bitter or unpleasant, but it happened, and they feel they have no power to change back to the way they used to be. Anger locked up inside changes personalities.

As a therapist, I am always encouraging people to get in touch with their anger, to acknowledge it, accept it, feel it and express it. It is much healthier to let anger out than to keep it in, to express it than to suppress it. But, of course, when a woman is in a relationship with an emotionally immature man, expressing anger is not as simple as therapists make it sound.

Many women have confided in me, over the years, that when they have attempted to express anger, their partner's response made everything much worse. What they expected was that the honest expression of their anger would be followed by a discussion which, in turn, would be followed by a resolution of the problem but, instead, all they experienced was more pain and more problems. Rather than accepting women's anger as an opportunity to talk things through and clear the air, men generally go into defensive mode whenever a woman expresses anger or annoyance or displeasure. It doesn't even seem to register with them that our expression of anger probably signifies that we are deeply unhappy about the way things are. All they seem to care about is how our anger makes them feel. They feel criticised and attacked, and all they care about at that moment is defending themselves.

A common form of defence used by men is attack. Many men interpret women's expression of anger as a personal attack on them and, they believe, any attack must be countered by a stronger attack. They attack verbally by yelling, threatening, using obscenities, humiliating their partners in front of others. They attack physically by intimidating, pushing, punching, kicking, raping—in other words, by criminal assault. Some men go so far as to defend against their partners' criticism by abusing or threatening to abuse the children. They know that this kind of attack will cause most mothers to back down immediately. The only aim of an immature man, in such situations, is to win. How he does it and who gets hurt along the way is of no concern to him.

The overtly aggressive response of defending against a perceived attack by attacking back is the preferred response of many immature men, but not all. There are those who prefer the more passive response of withdrawing. There is no speaking, no interacting, no affection, no sex, no acknowledgement at all of their partner's presence. And sometimes this passive-aggressive "assault" extends also to the children.

When such aggressive or passive-aggressive responses are the best women can expect from immature men, it is no wonder so many women decide to keep their anger to themselves. But I cannot say strongly enough that, regardless of men's responses, we must still find ways to express the anger we feel.

While anger is a normal emotion and ought to be a normal part of our interactions, it is probably the most misunderstood emotion we have. Many see it as a negative, unhealthy emotion when, in fact, it is a positive, healthy emotion. When it is expressed properly and received properly, it has amazing power to bring about healing. But most people seem to have difficulty relating to anger.

Women, in particular, have a strange relationship to anger. Most of us are conditioned from an early age to deny our angry feelings. While aggressive behaviour, swearing, yelling, throwing things around the room, are often tolerated in boys, they are strongly discouraged in girls. "Nice girls don't get angry." That's the message we grow up with. Consequently, many women believe anger has no place in their lives and work hard at controlling it. The discussion of anger, below, is designed to help us all understand it a little better and become more familiar with its function in our lives.

There are three options we all have in relation to our own anger. We can repress it, suppress it, or express it. The first is always bad for us; the second is mostly bad but not always; and the third is good for us, provided we do it in a way that is direct and appropriate.

Repression of anger

Repression is easiest understood when it is compared with suppression. In my discussion of "suppression" to follow, I will define suppression of anger as "keeping anger to ourselves". Repression of anger, in comparison, is "keeping anger *from* ourselves". In other words, repression allows us to fool ourselves into believing we never get angry. As such, it is much more damaging than suppression. It has the potential to cause serious psychological problems.

Most of us carry around with us repressed material from childhood. When children are subjected to unbearable experiences, the emotions connected with those experiences are often too frightening to deal with at such an early age. The psychological mechanism of repression enables a child to push the frightening emotions down and get on with life. The ability to repress events and feelings seems like a positive thing because it allows a child to cope in very difficult circumstances but, in the long-term, it is by no means positive. Repressed memories never completely go away. They are always there in a person's unconscious mind with the potential to cause problems. That is why, when you go to a therapist to talk about your depression or anxiety or eating disorder or whatever else, it is important that the therapist encourage you to talk about your past as well as your present. If there are repressed or semi-repressed memories contributing to your present discomfort, they must be released into consciousness, so that you can express and deal with the emotions which arise.

Repression is usually something which begins in childhood but it is by no means confined to childhood. In adult life, repression is common. Women, for example, repress anger all the time. After years of conditioning, many women "automatically" push their anger down inside them. It happens at an unconscious level, which means they don't even know they are doing it. This kind of automatic repression of anger is particularly insidious because it happens so quickly, each time, that the person is totally unaware of having had a feeling of anger at all.

So, when a woman says "I never feel angry", she is probably right. But that does not mean anger doesn't exist for her. It is a normal emotion that exists for everyone. Anger that is not felt or recognised or acknowledged does not go away. It stays inside and has the potential to cause serious physical and psychological problems.

Suppression of anger

While repression happens unconsciously and automatically, suppression is something we choose to do and is, therefore, not as psychologically damaging. When you suppress your anger, you are simply deciding to keep it to yourself rather than to express it.

If you are someone who chooses to keep your anger to yourself all the time, let me hasten to say before you become too pleased with yourself, that *it is not helpful to suppress anger all the time.* Such chronic passivity can also cause depression and other psychological and physical problems. If suppression is chosen at all, it must only occur occasionally and for good reason. The general rule is that anger ought to be expressed.

One of the unfortunate side effects of suppressing our anger is what is called "displacement", that is, placing or directing anger where it does not belong. A common example women often talk about is the experience of being angry at their husbands but suppressing it and then taking it out on their children. If your anger belongs to your partner, it is important that it be directed at him and not displaced on to your children.

Another example, which is probably even more common among women, is the experience of suppressing the anger we feel toward someone else and then turning it around and directing it at ourselves. When your partner puts you down, for example, and the anger welling up inside you clearly belongs to him, it is important not to displace that anger on to yourself. Women in such situations often blame themselves for being "silly" when, in fact, the blame belongs to their partners for their arrogant refusal to take women seriously. The displacing of anger is always a dishonest expression of anger. The honest and healthy thing to do is to express anger where it belongs.

Are there any guidelines to help one decide whether or not to suppress anger in any given situation? I don't know of any stated guidelines, but you may find helpful the guide I have developed for myself. In deciding whether to suppress or not to suppress anger in any given situation, I try to keep the following overall goal in mind: *to end every day without having stored up "unfinished business"*. There are times when I know that *suppressing* my anger will leave me feeling "unfinished" while, at other times, I know it is the *expression* of my anger that will leave me with unfinished business. Since it is unfinished business that causes us most of our problems, I personally find this an important criterion for judging whether or not, in any situation, I will express or not express the anger I feel.

Expression of anger
When making decisions between suppressing or expressing anger, remember that the decision to *express* your anger is usually the healthy choice. Also, it is the choice which gives relationships the optimum chance of being mature and healthy. There are two provisions, however, which must be adhered to if the expression of anger is to be a healthy option:

- It must be *direct* expression of anger.
- It must be *appropriate* expression of anger.

When we have the courage to express our anger directly, it minimises the need for us to express it indirectly and destructively. The most common ways anger is expressed in relationships include: sarcasm, joking, teasing, not listening, not speaking, moodiness, excessive demand for sex or lack of interest in sex. While these behaviours are not always indicators of suppressed anger, they often are and, as indirect expressions of anger, they are dishonest and destructive. Those who learn to express anger directly will have no need to resort to snide remarks, cheap shots, moody behaviour or sexual combat.

When you set your mind on developing the skill of expressing your anger directly, the only question left to be asked is: How? What is the appropriate expression of anger for you? The question of appropriateness has two parts to it. First, expression of anger must be appropriate to the situation and, second, it must be appropriate to your own personality.

While it is true, as I have said, that anger is a normal and natural emotion which occurs in us automatically when we experience frustration, powerlessness, intimidation, humiliation, abuse, injustice, it is important that we not allow the expression of our anger to be automatic. The way we express our anger, in any given situation, ought to be the way we have chosen. If we make it a matter of choice, then the way we express our anger is much more likely to be appropriate.

The following list of ways anger is expressed in our society represents the range of options from which we can choose:

Exploding

Exploding is often the way anger is expressed when it is allowed to happen spontaneously but, even after thinking about it, some people *choose* to express their anger in this way. They believe they cannot be satisfied that their anger has been expressed without exploding, that is, without yelling and screaming, without being abusive or violent or destructive. Although some couples claim to feel better after they have had a real knock-down, drag-out session, I personally find it difficult to see how such negative venting of anger can ever result in positive gains for any relationship. If it happened once and there was genuine reconciliation and renewed commitment, I could accept that the result could be positive, but the explosive venting of anger as a regular occurrence seems to me to be destructive.

Keeping it in

Many people, particularly women, choose to keep their anger in and allow the anger to express itself in sulking, withdrawing, martyr behaviour. Such suppression of anger is destructive of ourselves and our relationships.

Assertiveness

Speaking and acting assertively is the method, in my opinion, which allows for the most effective expression of anger. Assertiveness is the ability to speak up for oneself without resorting to aggressive and abusive behaviour. If you feel anger at another person because of something they said or did, you will say so. Assertiveness is having the courage to say what you think or feel in a way that is not destructive of anyone else.

Assertiveness is usually an indication that you respect yourself enough to believe that you are a worthwhile person, with worthwhile thoughts and opinions. You will talk about how you feel and what you think, and have an expectation that those you are talking to will listen. You will stand up for yourself, give your opinion, argue your point of view, speak honestly, express your anger and other emotions, and make decisions for your own life.

When you choose to be assertive, you are showing not only that you respect yourself but also that you respect other people. To be willing to be assertive with others, to be honest, to share your real self with them, to offer your opinions, to make your own decisions instead of helplessly relying on others to make decisions for you, are all signs that you respect the people you are interacting with.

Assertive behaviour is adult behaviour and, therefore, very healthy. But such behaviour on your part will not always be welcomed by immature men. An immature man almost always exhibits passive or aggressive behaviour and seems to feel most comfortable when you, too, are being passive or aggressive because he knows that when you respond passively or aggressively, he has won. Assertive behaviour from you shows that you are firmly in control of your own emotions and puts pressure on him to be more mature in his responses. He will not like that and will probably react defensively but, in the interests of developing a better relationship, it is important that you persevere.

An assertive woman calls on the strength that is within her. She speaks calmly and firmly. And she is persistent. In much of the literature on assertiveness training, the skill of persistence is called: the broken record. When what you say is ridiculed or dismissed, when you yourself are insulted or degraded, when you are met with tears or any similar red herring, you simply stand your ground and say it again. And again. And again. Assertive responses to situations are adult responses. (For a fuller discussion of assertiveness, see Situation 40.)

Counting to ten
Another method of expressing anger which is similar to the assertive method is that which is sometimes called "counting to ten". Another name for it is "time out".

The way it works is, when something happens which causes anger or displeasure to well up inside you, you immediately step away from it and give yourself time to calm down or get in control before going back and confronting the issue head on. Sometimes it is helpful to say something like: "I can't talk about this now. I need some time to calm down and get my thoughts in order. Let's talk about it in half-an-hour."

Taking time out in this way is a helpful technique for people who are trying to train themselves to respond assertively and to leave behind their old ways of responding passively or aggressively. The crucial thing to remember when choosing the "counting to ten" method is that you do come back and express your opinions and feelings. Time out is not to be taken as a convenient way of avoiding confrontation. When that happens, the healthy "counting to ten" method is turned into the unhealthy "keeping it in" method which is disastrous in terms of personal satisfaction and healthy relationships.

As you get better at the "counting to ten" method of expressing anger, you will find you need less and less time out before being able to confront an issue assertively. As you feel more comfortable with assertiveness as a method of response, you will find yourself responding assertively and appropriately to situations as they happen.

Withdrawing
While staying in a situation and withdrawing into a sulk is never helpful, there are some instances in which the decision to remove oneself altogether from a situation is the most healthy response one can make. There is much made in Western societies about the negative effect of "running away". The implication is that, no matter how awful a situation may be, no matter how long it has gone

on or how much you have engaged with it in an effort to change it, staying there is a sign of strength and withdrawing is a sign of weakness. I disagree. As I see it, to continue in a frustrating and destructive situation which shows no sign of ever changing is to acquiesce. Acquiescence, in such circumstances, is an act of weakness. Finding the courage to leave, on the other hand, is an act of strength.

If, after trying everything in your power to bring change to a bad situation—whether it be a damaging relationship, a frustrating job or a destructive social situation—there is absolutely nothing wrong with deciding to express your anger by walking away from it. Withdraw. Leave it behind you. Free yourself up to get on with your life.

Anger is better out than in. It is much more healthy for you to give expression to your anger than to keep it inside. It is up to you to decide which method of expression is most appropriate to any particular situation and, also, to your own personality. Occasionally, you will choose to explode but, most often, you will choose between assertiveness, counting to ten, or withdrawing from a situation altogether.

Boy-power

14. Living with a bully

Living with a man who is a bully is not a pleasant experience. Such a man is not unlike the bully-boys who menace most schoolyards. Occasionally a schoolyard bully is a girl, but most often it is a boy. Those who have studied the phenomenon of bullying in schools report that the victims of girls' bullying are usually other girls, while boys' victims are both girls and boys. The boys who are victimised by boys are usually those who are perceived to be weaker. Girls' bullying often takes the form of excluding someone from the group, ostracising her, calling her names. Boys who are bullies tend to tease and intimidate and ridicule, push and shove and punch. Bully-boys enjoy challenging others, dominating others, humiliating others.

There doesn't seem to be anything planned or rational about the way bullies act, whether the bully is a child or an adult. They just see an occasion to exercise power over others and do it spontaneously. While bullying is a totally inadequate way of relating to others, it seems to be the only way some people know.

Some men seem actually to begin their bullying behaviour once they are married or living with a woman. They perceive their partner and children as weaker than themselves and, therefore, easy to bully. Other men seem to be simply continuing the behaviour they used in their childhood. Of course, it would be better for adult relationships if such behaviour were conditioned out of children as soon as it begins but, while that is exactly what happens with most girl-bullies, some boys are allowed to continue. Parents may try but, after initial attempts fail, most are inclined to give up and find justification in the belief that "boys will be boys". In other words, bullying is "natural" to boys, they decide, so why fight it?

If bullying is not "natural" for boys, which it isn't, we have to go on to ask: Where does the tendency for bullying come from? How do children learn such behaviour?

There are two main experiences that contribute to a child's adopting bullying behaviour. The first is *the bullying behaviour of parents toward them*. Some parents have the mistaken view that the way to ensure their children "know who's boss", the way to engender obedience and good behaviour in children, is to bully them. Parents who relate to their children by bullying, dominating, intimidating and humiliating them will, without a doubt, raise children who have problems. Some will grow up to be timid, fearful, anxious teenagers and adults, while others will grow up to be bullying, intimidating, violent teenagers and adults. In other words, if the first experience children have of relating to others is that of being bullied, they will either shrink from relationships or relate by bullying.

The other factor which contributes to a child's becoming a bully is *the example of parents, teachers and other adults*. This refers to a situation where children may not, themselves, be bullied by adults but are living in an atmosphere of bullying. When they see it, when they experience others being bullied (whether at home or school), it becomes a familiar way of relating. Any behaviour which is familiar is easy for a child to emulate. A moment of great sadness for women who are bullied by their husbands is when they first notice their sons relating to their siblings in the same bullying way. Even more distressing is when those sons follow their father's example and begin bullying their mother, showing her the same lack of respect she has endured from him.

It follows, then, that adults can reduce the amount of bullying behaviour children learn by reducing our own bullying behaviour toward them and each other. This does not mean allowing children to do as they like. It means that we will set a better example and learn better ways of giving them advice or more considered ways of punishing them when we think they would gain by it.

Although an understanding of how bullying behaviour may begin in people is interesting, it remains that such behaviour is inexcusable. Knowing how your partner's behaviour may have developed does not mean you ought to excuse him. A bully will never improve his behaviour by having that behaviour excused or condoned. Always remember: *adults can change behaviour learned in childhood—if they want to*. A bully can change his behaviour if he wants to, but he will only *want* to if he no longer gets from it the feeling of power he craves. Put pressure on him to stop. Don't be intimidated by him.

Suggestions for action

The first two suggestions have already been mentioned above:

Don't excuse him

Understanding why he does it and making excuses for him will not result in his changing his behaviour. Let him know that his behaviour is unacceptable and must stop.

Don't be intimidated by his bullying

This is easy to say but not always easy to do. If there is a danger that his bullying words will turn to actual physical violence, you need to be the judge of how you respond. However, it is important that you see his bullying for what it is—a pathetic attempt by a weak man to make himself feel powerful.

Respond assertively

If you are able to respond assertively, that is, if there is little or no fear of violence, there are two steps that are often effective:

1. Tell him how you feel about his bullying behaviour and that you want it to stop.
2. If it doesn't stop, show by your confident behaviour that your self-esteem is not weakened by his threats. Look him straight in the eye when he bullies you. When you respond to him, speak with confidence. Walk with your head held high. Practise what we call "assertive ignoring", that is, construct a psychic barrier around yourself which gives out a clear message: Don't come near me!

Most bullies are spurred on by cowering behaviour in their victims. If you develop an assertive manner and practise assertive ignoring, you will deprive him of the satisfaction of thinking he has intimidated you. When the "fun" goes out of it or the feeling of power is no longer there, most bullies change their behaviour. This is not to say their behaviour gets better but, at least, it provides an opportunity for something better to emerge.

[Postcard] Jacky Fleming (1992). *Where's my dinner?*
Leeds: Jacky Fleming Cartoons.

15. When you are the victim of physical abuse

Almost every day I see or hear something which reminds me of how commonplace violence against women is in our society and how easily ordinary people seem to accept it as a "natural" part of life. Yesterday, I was driving along in my car listening to the radio. One of my favourite announcers was talking and, as a way of introducing some music he was about to play, he told a story which he referred to as a "beautiful" legend. Apparently developed by a certain culture as a way of explaining the existence of stars in the sky, it went something like this:

The male image in the story desperately wanted to share his life with the female image who lived in the water. But, whenever he went near her, she would dive under the water and swim away from him. One day he caught her, "captured" her (that was the word the radio announcer used). As he captured her, she kicked the water so hard that a great burst of stars appeared and floated up to the sky. He took her away to live with him beyond the stars. What a "lovely" story!

I used to think legends like that were enchanting until I began looking at them from the point of view of the women in the stories. In this particular legend, the woman clearly did not want to be with him. He stalked her. She hid from him. She did everything she could to get away from him. In the end, he got his own way. Notice that he didn't attempt to woo her. He didn't present himself in such a way that she eventually fell in love with him and went with him willingly. No. He "captured" her. He kidnapped her. He took her against her will. This is an extremely violent act. And, when we hear a story like this and think of it only as a story about how stars were created, we say: "What a lovely story."

Violence against women is not "a lovely story", no matter how it might be dressed up. Women who live in relationships with men who are violent will tell you the experience can be called a lot of things: heart-breaking, frightening, confusing, demeaning, destructive—but never "lovely".

If you are living in a relationship with a violent man, you must wonder sometimes how you came to be in that situation. If you grew up in a violent household, you were probably not so much *shocked* by your partner's first assault on you, as very disappointed. You had hoped that your relationship would be different but now you see it starting down the same track as that endured by your mother. If you did not grow up with violence, if you are one of those women for whom domestic violence was something you had heard about but never witnessed you, no doubt, did experience shock the first time you were assaulted by your partner. You found it hard to believe that the man you loved, the man you made a commitment with, the man who said he loved you, would treat you that way.

Once male violence occurs in a relationship, it often follows a pattern which some researchers have called a "cycle of violence". The pattern, or cycle, goes like this:

1. A man assaults his partner.
2. The woman is devastated. She is confused. She tries desperately to work out what went wrong.
3. The man is, then, full of remorse. He's so sorry. He doesn't know what came over him. He'll never do it again.
4. The woman wants to believe it was an aberration. She wants to believe that his violent behaviour was so totally out of character that he will never do it again.

5. They analyse the situation together. Often the man succeeds in convincing the woman that she was partly or largely to blame for his violence. If only she hadn't said this or done that. If only she had been more considerate. If only she hadn't been twenty minutes late getting dinner on the table. If only she hadn't got pregnant. If only she hadn't asked him to turn the TV down. *It is quite common, at this stage, for the guilt to be turned around. Instead of the perpetrator of the violence taking the blame and feeling guilty, it is the victim who accepts the blame and takes on the guilt.* She apologises to him and promises she'll try hard to change!

6. Things settle down. She is careful not to provoke him and he gets on with his life as if nothing happened.

7. Before long, the man's frustration begins to grow again. As his frustration grows, so his anger grows and it isn't long before he is violent again.

I want to emphasise here that it is absolutely pointless for a woman to take the blame for her partner's violence and to walk around on eggshells trying not to upset him, because *the frustration he feels comes from within himself.* It wouldn't matter how perfect his partner was, he would still experience frustration and find a way to blame her. The cycle begins again. He is violent. He is sorry. You find a way to blame yourself again. You forgive him. You both promise to try harder and are determined it will never happen again. And so it goes on and on, around and around.

A tragic fact about violence in relationships is that both partners are affected in ways which make it easy for the violence to continue. Every time a man is violent towards his partner, it becomes easier for him to repeat.

Violence becomes more familiar. Also, there is no longer any need for him to fear the consequences. He got away with it all those other times, so he can be fairly certain what the outcome will be. He feels stronger and more self-assured. A woman who is a victim of her partner's violence, conversely, gets weaker with every occasion of violence. Accepting his violence in the past weakens her in the sense that it makes every subsequent episode easier to accept. The damage to her self-esteem and self-confidence, each time, makes it more and more difficult for her to find the courage to leave.

If you are in a relationship with a violent man, you will already know that, soon after the first assault, your life began to revolve around your partner's violence. Everything you say, every one of your mannerisms, every decision you make, everything about your life is analysed and organised by you with reference to whether or not he will be upset and his violence reappear. Such a life can never be relaxed or spontaneous or fulfilling. It's a nightmare. A half-life. And I urge you to get off the treadmill and claim your own life again.

Suggestions for action

Leave him

Give him a second chance, if you like, but as soon as he assaults you a second time, you must leave him. No ifs or buts. Studies into domestic violence show very clearly that when men begin to assault their partners, their violence usually escalates. They become more violent rather than less. Don't be fooled by your partner's expressions of remorse or his promises never to do it again. They mean nothing unless he follows them up by actually seeking help from a professional person. To take the step of going to a therapist—not just once, but for a period of time—is a sign that he seriously wants to stop. Many men *say* they will go and talk to a counsellor and, on that basis, their partners agree to stay with them, only to find that they never actually get around to making an appointment. Some women think they will help out by phoning and making an appointment for their violent partner who feigns remorse and says he will do "anything" to make it up to her. Anything, that is, except keep the appointment she made for him. The truth is that perpetrators of violence in the home rarely seek help to curb their violence unless they are forced to do so by the police. Why is that?

I always used to think that men who were violent in the home probably didn't *want* to be. It was probably just that something came over them and they exploded and found themselves behaving in a way that they really didn't want to. After years of experience as a therapist and years of studying the issue of domestic violence, I am now of the opinion that men assault their partners because they want to. There is a slogan I've seen on car bumper stickers which says: "Men who use violence, choose violence." I agree. It is a choice they make. If they really were stunned by their violent behaviour, they would go immediately in search of help and wouldn't rest until they found the kind of help they needed. They wouldn't have to be reminded or cajoled or urged or threatened. It must be said that a man who resists or refuses to get outside help to understand the factors contributing to his tendency to violence, is not serious about wanting to ensure that it doesn't happen again. He is violent because he *wants* to be violent. If this is your situation, you must leave him.

Give top priority to your safety and the safety of your children

If you do decide, after the first assault, that you will stay, be aware of the danger you and your children are in. Don't be naïve about it. Don't close your eyes to the fact that you are choosing to stay in a "war zone" in which the enemy could attack at any time. Plan an escape route so that if/when it happens again, you will not be caught by surprise. Make sure your plan is one that can be put into action without delay.

Don't take the blame for his violence

Why do so many women take the blame for relationship problems which are very obviously not their fault? One of the reasons, I believe, is that it makes a problem appear more manageable. If the blame is focused on the one who is actually causing the problem and that person refuses to take responsibility for his behaviour, then there is no room to move. A woman is stuck in a situation which has no chance of being resolved. But if it can be turned around so that she can blame herself for the problem, then she feels as if there is hope. Many women are pleased, therefore, to accept responsibility for their partner's violence because they can then convince themselves that there is light at the end of the tunnel. All they have to do is change their own behaviour and the problem will be resolved.

Don't do it! Don't take the blame for something you didn't do. It will only make the situation worse in the long run. Remember, an immature man has the ethics of a rebellious little boy. If he can pass the blame off on to someone else, he will gladly do so. Then he is free to continue his bad behaviour. The only hope for change in

Judy Horacek (1992/2003). *Life on the Edge.*
Melbourne: Spinifex, p. 27.

his behaviour is if he is made to shoulder the blame, made to face up to what he has done, made to admit that his violence is entirely his responsibility.

So, it doesn't matter what you did prior to his assault on you. You may have made fun of him, criticised him, even yelled at him, and it may well be that you wish you hadn't acted the way you did, but be careful not to construe that as meaning you were to blame for his violence. Regardless of what you did, his violence is his responsibility.

Don't make excuses for his violence

When a man chooses to assault his partner, there is absolutely no excuse for it. But, whenever a woman is assaulted by the man she loves, the first thing she does is try to figure out why it happened. She searches desperately for excuses or "reasons" so that she doesn't have to face the fact that the reason he assaulted her was simply that he wanted to. Such a truth is too painful to bear. The most common excuses women come up with are:

- he had a terrible childhood
- his mother treated him really badly
- he was sexually abused by his father/grand-father/uncle/cousin . . .
- he's had a lot of stress at work
- the noise the children make really stresses him out
- he can't stand the baby crying all the time
- he doesn't get as much sex as he wants.

There is absolutely no excuse for violence, and there is especially no excuse for violence in the home. One's home is supposed to be one's haven, a safe place.

For many women and children, however, it is the most dangerous place on earth.

Don't look for excuses for a man's violence. The truth is that, for as long as he is excused, he will continue to be violent. If you have decided not to leave your partner, then the only hope you and your children have lies in his accepting full responsibility for his violence. If he has problems from his past or in the present, it is his responsibility to get some help to deal with those pressures. He has absolutely no right to take out his frustrations on you.

Stop making excuses for him. It's your only hope.

16. When you see your partner's behaviour emerging in your son

One of the saddest, most degrading scenarios I can ever imagine is that of a mother being physically and/or sexually abused by her child. I don't like reminding myself that such situations do exist. It hurts too much to think that women have to endure such humiliation. But abuse by one's own teenage or adult child does happen and, since it does exist, we must have the courage to talk about it. Why? Because if we ever hope to eradicate this sad and sorry phenomenon from our society, we must first acknowledge that it happens.

Maybe you are one of those women suffering at the hands of your son. Occasionally, teenage girls physically abuse their mothers, but the perpetrators are overwhelmingly sons following in the footsteps of their fathers or step-fathers.

What a confusing situation for you to be in. You carried this boy in your womb. You endured the pain of childbirth. You loved and cared for him as well as you could. You protected him from the violence of your partner/s as much as possible. You sacrificed yourself in so many ways. And now . . .

There are those who look at the violence of the animal world and say that violence in humans must be natural. It must be part of our genetic make-up as human animals and all we can do, they say, is learn to live with it. I don't accept that argument at all, for the simple reason that male animals are very seldom violent toward their mate or their offspring. If human violence did follow the pattern of animal violence, we would see male violence almost exclusively occurring against other males and female violence almost exclusively in the protection of their young. Male violence against women and children seems to be a *human* phenomenon. Far from being "natural", then, it seems that male violence against women and children is learned behaviour.

A boy's violence toward his mother isn't a natural thing. It isn't something that has to happen in the sense that it can't be avoided. Rather, it is learned behaviour and, as suggested in Situation 14, it is most probably learned through the example of adult men with whom he has lived.

When children live in a situation where their mother is regularly abused verbally and/or physically, they automatically learn that their mother is not worthy of respect. She's just a punching bag. She's there to be criticised and dumped on. Taken a step further, some boys learn, not just that their mother is someone who can be abused whenever they feel like it, but also that *all* women are unworthy of respect. All women exist to be intimidated and abused by men. Girls, on the other hand, learn that women should expect to be abused, that male abuse of women is an inevitable part of life and that, when it happens to them, they ought to accept it and learn how to live with it. The father's arrogance and violence are passed on to his sons while the woman's sense of hopelessness and low self-esteem are passed on to her daughters.

While the incidence of boys physically and sexually abusing their mothers is growing, it is still more common to hear of boys physically and sexually abusing their sisters and other girls. Influenced by their father's attitude which gives a clear message that women and girls exist to be used and abused, some boys become perpetrators of violence against women and girls at an early age, while others simply become insufferably arrogant and self-absorbed.

Suggestions for action

What should you do when you see your partner's behaviour emerging in your son?

Take your children and leave

By the time you actually recognise that your son is imitating his father's arrogant attitude or violent behaviour, it is almost too late to do anything to prevent it from developing. But you must do what you can to separate your boy from your partner's negative influence.

Knowing that violence in all its forms (emotional, physical and sexual), once introduced into a relationship, escalates rather than diminishes, it is strongly advised that you leave a violent man after his first attack on you. If you feel you want to give him one more chance, then do that, but only *one* more chance. As soon as the second assault on you occurs, take the children and leave. If your self-esteem is so low that you can't bring yourself to do it for your own sake, then do it for the sake of your children.

A major concern for many women contemplating leaving their marriage is the issue of economic survival. It is known that some men, incensed by their partner's decision to leave, go to extraordinary lengths to avoid paying maintenance or providing any assistance at all toward the support of their children. There is no doubt that leaving a financially secure situation for one that is unknown is a big step for you to take. On the positive side, many women attest to the fact that the support networks set up in recent years in the form of women's refuges and women's centres, as well as government support through sole parents' benefit and child support, have enabled them to survive until such time as they were able to support themselves.

Don't let the fear of financial hardship keep you in a relationship that is unhealthy and unsafe for you and your children. You *will* survive, and you will all be much happier.

Look for positive male role-models for your children to have contact with

Mothers have to be really careful these days in terms of the men they allow near their children, but there are some good men out there if you take the time to find them. Whatever you do, don't leave your children, girls or boys, in the care of a teenage or adult male unless you know you can trust him totally. Contact with emotionally mature men who know how to relate to children in a positive way can only be good for your children.

Work on improving your own self-esteem

If you have been a victim of violence, even just once, your self-esteem has been damaged. The longer you stayed in that relationship, the more your self-esteem would have plummetted. Now that you are out of the relationship, you are free to discover yourself all over again. The more you get to know your true self, the more you will feel at peace with the world and the more you will be able to present an example to your children of an adult whose self-esteem and confidence are intact. (For a discussion of how to go about enhancing your self-esteem, see Situation 38.)

17. When you are the victim of sexual abuse

Sexual abuse takes many forms, some of which will be discussed in the following pages. In Situations 17 to 24, we will look at rape, intimidation, rough sex, sexual experimentation, abandonment, sexual harassment, childhood sexual abuse and pornography.

Do you ever feel like an object for your partner's sexual gratification? Many relationships begin with sex which seems fairly equal—equal desire, equal enjoyment—but degenerate into a situation where one partner feels used by the other. Sex ought to be something two people do together, a shared experience, an activity in which two people give pleasure to each other and the enjoyment is mutual. It is important to emphasise that it doesn't always have to mean *equal* enjoyment, simply because it is often the case that one partner gets more pleasure from a particular sexual encounter than the other (due to other factors such as levels of tiredness, etc.) but there must be pleasure in it for both.

Here, I want to examine those relationships where sex cannot be said to be a mutual, shared activity, and focus particularly on the problems of rape, intimidation, rough sex and sexual experimentation.

Rape has been described as "having sex with someone when you know that person doesn't want it". According to this definitiion, most men are guilty of raping their partners at some time in their lives and most women are guilty of passively consenting to rape.

Rape in marriage, or rape in relationships, occurs in more serious ways as well. While it is serious for a man to have sex with a woman when he senses she doesn't want it, it is even more serious to have sex when she actually says "no". This is rape in the legal sense. A man who forces himself on his partner in this way can and should be prosecuted for rape. Some women describe their experience of married life as that of being subjected to the pain and humiliation of rape on a daily basis. How is it that so many men believe sex is their right? I suppose the church has contributed to this belief with its emphasis on "conjugal rights". In other words, marriage confers on couples (and, in practice, that usually means men) the right to have sex whether their partner wants it or not. One wonders why the term "conjugal rights" has never been interpreted to include the right to say no! The same can be said of the church's term "marital obliga-tion". Why is that term never interpreted to mean the obligation to refrain from sex until both partners want it? The answer is obvious. It is because the terms "conju-gal rights" and "marital obligation" were invented by men!

Some women say that, while they have never felt that their partners had raped them, they do often feel intim-idated into having sex. They experience a man's erect penis, and the way he goes about making sure his partner knows he has an erection, as really intimidating.

Emotionally immature men aren't renowned for their sophisticated techniques when it comes to love-making. Some seem to think that as soon as they get an erection, the whole world has to stop and pay attention. They seem to want praise for how big it is or how hard it is or how clever they are. Some poke their partner in the back with it thinking, I suppose, that she will be turned on by this wonderfully erotic technique and will roll over and fall helplessly into his arms, saying "Take me, take me!" Other men seem to need to talk dirty in order to excite themselves and, then, once they manage an erection, they are so proud of it and so excited by it that their crude talk escalates to a point where their partner feels dirty. She is intimidated by his talk. At that moment, she would rather be a hundred miles away; instead, she consents to sex because she knows that will stop the crude talk and behaviour till the next time and, also, it will stop the intimidation she feels.

Men who have immature attitudes toward sex don't usually make love. They have sex. And, more to the point, they have self-gratifying sex (sex for themselves). In addition to rape and intimidation, the other two expressions of immature attitudes toward sex mentioned above are: rough sex and sexual experimentation.

There is a school of thought which maintains that women enjoy rough sex. Women, they say, are masochistic by nature, that is, they get pleasure out of being hurt. Pain in sex turns them on. Have you ever heard of anything so ridiculous? Once again, I'm sure you can guess that it was a man who came up with that theory! Of course, I won't deny there are women who say they like it a bit rough, and there are also those who get off on sado-masochistic (S-M) fantasies and games, but the overwhelming majority of women do not want to be hurt in sex. They want it to be an expression of love and/or an enjoyable, shared experience between equals. If your partner has a need to be rough, tell him to save that till he's masturbating! He can be as rough as he likes with himself but, when he's with you, you want passion and gentleness and genuine intimacy.

Finally, there are those men who insist on experimenting. They want to try out different forms of sex and you are the guinea pig used in the experiments. Of course, there is nothing wrong with sexual experiment-ation so long as both partners want to make some changes and so long as the experimenting doesn't include things that exploit and degrade one or both of you. But, more often than not, it is the man in the partnership who wants to experiment and the woman who is used, sometimes with her grudging consent, sometimes without her consent.

Sexual experimentation is often prompted by a man's desire to try out some of the things he has seen in pornographic magazines or videos and, since pornography exploits women in a major way, women who go along with their partner's desire to experiment are certain to be exploited, used, degraded. Milder, but no less degrading, forms of experimentation include that of a man seeing how long he can go without ejaculating. What used to be normal intercourse—a sexual activity enjoyed by two people—is turned into a contest between the man and his penis. The woman as person doesn't exist. She becomes a vagina, a hole, a vehicle used to carry out the man's experiment.

Other forms of experimentation include partner-swapping, sex involving a third person, group sex, and so on. Hailed in the 1970s as sexually liberating forms of experimentation, most of these kinds of experiments ended in separation and divorce. The same is true today. There are still people who think sex with others will spice up their sex-lives with their partners, but the reality is that such experiments usually destroy any hope that sex will be a mutual and satisfying expression of love between two people.

If sex with your partner leaves you feeling you have been raped, if you feel intimidated, if you feel you are treated more roughly than you want, or if you feel you are being used for his experimentation, then you must face the fact that you are a victim of sexual abuse. Once you allow yourself to admit that, you will be a step closer to saying "no" to unwanted sexual advances and, also, a step closer to insisting on the kind of sex-life that you can enjoy.

Suggestions for action

Refuse to be a victim of sexual abuse

Remember that an immature man will keep abusing you for as long as he can get away with it. It's important, therefore, that you take time by yourself thinking through the whole issue of sex and making some decisions about what you want rather than settling for the role of victim. What do you want? If your sex-life could be just as you wanted it, what would it be like? When I ask women that question in therapy, lots of them say: "I'd have no sex at all." Naturally, if sex presents huge problems for a woman in her relationship, she will spend time fantasising a situation where there are absolutely no demands for sex and, indeed, no sex. Other women respond to the question with detailed descriptions of their fantasies about loving, passionate, exciting sex. Others say they have never really thought about it. They see sex as something to be resisted or endured.

I recommend that you spend some time working out how you would like it to be, because the only way you are going to be able to stop feeling like and actually being a victim of sexual abuse, is to refuse to do any of the degrading things your partner wants and insist on a new way. You have to work out what you want that new way to be before you can insist on it.

I realise there's no guarantee that an immature, self-serving man will listen to you but, at least, it's worth a try. If your partner prefers to continue sexually abusing you, remember that he's doing it because he likes it that way, and you ought to consider leaving him.

Say "no" if you mean "no"

A marriage licence is not a licence to rape. It does not give men the right to have sex whenever they want it. It does not give them the right to have sex with you against your will. Also, it does not mean you are under an obligation to satisfy his sexual needs. It has been said so often by men that "When a woman says no, she means maybe." Often it is said as a joke but, sadly, there are men who convince themselves that it's true as a way of justifying the fact they they forced themselves on to their partner and had sex with her knowing that she didn't want it.

I am not wanting to imply that men are slow to understand, of course, but on those occasions when you do not want sex, it is important that you say "no" as clearly as possible. This will not always save you from rape but, at least, your partner will not be able to justify his actions by blaming you for giving mixed messages. A clearly stated "no" means "no".

Insist that your sexual relationship be a shared experience between equals

Again, I must say that insisting on a more equal sexual relationship in which there is pleasure for both partners, will not guarantee that it will be so. But, if your partner is one of those many, many men who are secretly insecure about sex, there is a chance that your saying what you want and how you think it can be achieved will give him the guidance he needs and improve his confidence in this area. Don't expect that he will *tell* you that he is insecure, of course, or that he has taken any notice of what you've said, but it may help.

Don't agree to any sexual activity that doesn't feel right

Some women, wanting to please their partners, find themselves agreeing to sexual experimentation that they would really rather not do. Don't do it! Why? Because, when you engage in sex that makes you feel bad, dirty, exploited or degraded, it isn't long before you begin putting up a psychological barrier to sex of any kind. You find yourself looking for excuses so that you don't have to have sex at all. Whenever your partner gives the slightest indication that he would like to make love/have sex, your barrier goes up automatically. You get to the stage where you don't even want him to hug you or kiss you or show any affection at all because of your fear that it might progress to sex. Agreeing to sexual activity that doesn't feel right to you is the first step in undermining your enjoyment of sex and turning yourself off.

Whatever you do, refuse to be complicit in your own sexual abuse.

Jacky Fleming (1992). *Never Give Up*. London: Penguin.

18. When you have sex to keep the peace

Sex is supposed to be an expression of love. There are endless books describing how sex brings two people together and cements their relationship. Sex, we're told, provides excitement, passion, immense pleasure and a feeling that "all's right with the world".

I wonder who wrote those books. Certainly not any woman living in a relationship with a man who acts like a boy. Sex is supposed to be an activity two people engage in *when they both want it*. If one partner wants it and the other doesn't, then it must not occur. But, with an immature man, every rejection of his approaches for sex is met with an extreme reaction.

First, there are those who sulk. Sometimes the sulk goes on for days, or even weeks. He doesn't speak. Won't do anything around the house. Keeps to himself. All the while he's engaging in this silent protest, he's hoping his partner is getting the message that she has it in her power to make him "happy". Of course, as soon as they do have sex again, he's happy. In the early months or years of a relationship, it takes a woman a while to figure out that her simple "no" to sex has been the cause of his moods. Some women, on figuring that out, decide that saying yes more often is a whole lot easier than putting up with his sulking. But having sex to keep one's partner in a good mood makes a woman feel similar to a prostitute. She knows in her heart that, just as prostitutes exchange sex for money, she has exchanged sex for a more pleasant atmosphere around the house.

Second, there are those men who become angry and abusive. A simple "no" to his suggestion of sex causes an immediate explosion of anger and a tirade of abuse. He calls his partner anything from frigid to a slut. Accuses her of having it off with everyone in the neighbourhood. She's selfish, only thinks about herself, doesn't care about his needs. And so it goes on. Again, this is a situation in which a woman learns to calculate the positives and negatives of saying no to sex. Many decide that it is easier to say yes than to deal with the consequences of saying no.

A third group of men are those who respond to rejection with actual physical violence. They may not be violent every time, but it is enough to ensure that their partner develops a fear of the consequences of her "no". It doesn't take women in these situations long to calculate that it is probably easier, and safer, to give in and have sex.

What a destructive role sex plays in the lives of men who give no thought to what it must be like for their partners when they are forced to prostitute themselves in order to satisfy men's demands for sex. If you are in a situation where your partner sulks, or becomes angry and abusive, or perpetrates violence against you whenever you say no to sex, make up your mind that you will not stay indefinitely in such a destructive situation. You may not be able to leave yet but, at least, take time to think about what you want for your life and make yourself a promise that, one day, you will take steps to create a better life for yourself.

Suggestions for action

Don't prostitute yourself for anyone

I realise that the threat of violence may mean you have to agree, at times, to have sex with your partner when you don't want to but, short of the threat of violence, it is better for you if you don't consent to sex merely to keep the peace. Look for other ways to deal with the sulking, the anger and the abusive talk. Every time your partner's unacceptable behaviour is rewarded with the sex he is demanding, it will provide the incentive for him to continue behaving in those ways. He will keep behaving like a spoilt child until the behaviour stops working for him.

Seek out a Women's Centre or a female counsellor

Women living in these kinds of situations often experience confusion, shame and a deep sense of loneliness, and it helps greatly if there is someone to confide in. It isn't always easy or desirable to talk to a friend or relative about matters as intimate as how you feel about having sex simply to keep the peace. So, I strongly suggest you look for a counsellor who will be supportive and empathic. Go to a Women's Centre or find a female counsellor, therapist or psychologist, preferably one who comes highly recommended. Why do I stress that it ought to be a woman? Because in matters of sex, men can have no idea what it is like for a woman, in the same way as women have no idea what it is like for a man. A woman will be much more likely to provide the empathy and support you need. If the first counsellor you try doesn't seem to be on the same wavelength as you, then try another. Shop around till you find someone you feel comfortable talking to.

19. Being abandoned after sex

Not all emotionally immature men are self-centred in bed. As a matter of fact, some women tell me sex is the best part of their relationship. It's the reason they stay. Sex is important to them and good sex is hard to find. Among those women who enjoy sex with their partner, however, there are some who speak of feeling abandoned as soon as it is over. It's that feeling of abandonment that I want to focus on here.

A closer look at what happens when two people make love reveals that the period immediately after climax or orgasm is a time when both partners can feel vulnerable. You both enter into the love-making, "give" yourselves, risk yourselves and, when it's over, you sometimes need to feel reassured. I don't mean you need verbal reassurance about your performance in bed. No, I'm talking about a few moments of closeness when you still feel very focused on each other. That brief time when you share the experience of coming down from a sexual high is a time when the bond between you is strengthened.

Lots of people, women and men, have the experience of feeling abandoned after sex. Some women are in the habit of jumping out of bed as soon as intercourse is over and going to the bathroom, leaving their partner to deal with his feelings alone. Similarly, some men are in the habit of rolling over and going to sleep immediately after intercourse, leaving their partner alone with her thoughts and feelings. I don't mean to imply that everyone feels alone and abandoned when one partner leaves the scene immediately after sex. Most couples have developed their routines. They do what they do and neither partner would want those routines to change. But, when one partner does consistently feel abandoned after sex, it is crucial that the problem be addressed.

Sex researchers, over the years, have pointed out that there are three important stages in love-making. The first stage is commonly called "foreplay". Isn't that an interesting word? It implies that all the kissing and touching and stroking a couple does before intercourse is not really sex. It's foreplay. It's what you do *before* sex. Now such a term can only have been coined by a man! Men are much more likely to believe that intercourse is the real thing and that what you do before or after intercourse is a kind of adjunct to the real thing. For women, on the other hand, sex begins the moment signals are sent out and reciprocated. When a woman freely chooses to have sex with her partner, all the touching and petting before intercourse is just as enjoyable, exciting, satisfying as the intercourse itself. Indeed, many women say it is the best part of a sexual encounter and that they only go on to intercourse because they know it is what their partner finds most enjoyable, exciting, satisfying.

The second stage is intercourse and/or climax or orgasm. And the third stage of love-making is the "resolution" stage, that is, the period after climax when the two people involved experience a resolving or settling down both physically and emotionally. It is during this time, researchers say, that both partners can experience a cementing and a confirmation of their love for each other and, consequently, a strengthening of the relationship.

Suggestions for action

Analyse your own love-making behaviour

If you are one of those women who avoids stage three in the love-making process by leaving the scene immediately after intercourse and if, on reflection, you think it may be possible that your partner feels abandoned, talk to him about it. If he says everything is all right the way it is, then accept his word and continue doing what you've always done. If he indicates he would like to spend a few quiet minutes with you before going to sleep, then you may want to change your routine a little.

I don't want to ignore the fact that some women have good reason to get up immediately after intercourse. They do it as a way of giving their partner the message that sex is over and it's time to go to sleep. These women have learned, over the years, that their partner will never stop of his own accord. Like a little boy, he never allows himself to experience satisfaction. He wants more and more, and wonders why he gets less and less. If you are in a situation like that then, by all means, continue the practice that works for you. Don't allow your partner to spoil a good experience of sex by prolonging it to a point where you could be turned off sex for life.

If you feel abandoned after sex,
talk to your partner about it

If it is your partner who gets up and leaves, or rolls over and goes to sleep immediately after he has ejaculated, leaving you feeling abandoned, then it is important that you talk to him about how you feel. Men who aren't interested in talking about anything, especially anything of concern to you, will either brush you aside or take it as a criticism and turn it into World War III. If that is how your partner normally responds to your attempts at talking, then you will be prepared for it.

If he prides himself on being a good lover, then he will probably take notice of what you say (even if he won't give you the satisfaction of having a normal conversation about it!) and you may notice some change. It's crucial, though, that you not be too "demanding" in terms of intimate time spent together. Just as some men try to prolong good sex, some women try to prolong any experience of closeness with their partner because it's so rare. You only need a few minutes of "resolution" after intercourse, so be careful not to try to extend it to half an hour or an hour. As I said before in relation to men, if you try to get more and more, you'll end up with less and less.

When you attempt to speak to your partner about feelings of abandonment after intercourse, he will respond in one of four ways:

1. He will listen, take your feelings seriously, and make permanent changes to his after-intercourse habits.
2. He will, as described above, refuse to discuss it, but make some changes anyway.
3. He will make changes but, as is often the case with immature men, those changes will last only for a week or so and he will then revert to his old habits.
4. He will refuse to listen and refuse to change.

Let's hope your attempt at talking to your partner has positive results. If it doesn't, and if you continue to feel abandoned after sex, you may want to change your way of dealing with those feelings. One suggestion is that, instead of lying in bed feeling sad and lonely and angry in response to his rolling over and going to sleep, you develop the habit of getting up and sitting quietly in another room for a brief time (reading or meditating in some way) and then go back to bed when you're relaxed and ready to go to sleep.

20. When you are a victim of sexual harassment in your own home

We've heard a lot in recent years about sexual harassment in the workplace. It ranges from suggestive comments and unwanted touching to actual rape. Occasionally the victim of sexual harassment is a man, but most often it is a woman. The perpetrator can be a woman but it is usually a man.

Men who harass women at work create a situation where just the thought of having to go to work can be a source of great anxiety for the victims. Some women report their harassment to management while others prefer to battle through on their own. When it is reported, responsible managers usually approach the perpetrator and warn him that his harassment must stop, but there are other managers who simply treat the whole issue as a joke, "a bit of fun". Of course, it is often the manager himself who is the perpetrator. Most victims feel so powerless and, in some cases, embarrassed, that they don't report the harassment to anybody. They hold on as long as they can, some because they enjoy their work and object to being put in a position where they have to consider leaving, and some because other employment is difficult to find. All victims of sexual harassment who don't report the harassment or take other steps to make it stop, will eventually leave.

Sexual harassment in the workplace is still largely a hidden problem and, consequently, the extent of it is unknown. Exactly the same can be said of sexual harassment in the home. It is a hidden problem. Women who are sexually harassed by their partners are usually embarrassed by it and prefer not to tell anyone, so there is no way of knowing how prevalent it is. What therapists and counsellors know is that it is far more prevalent than most people realise, and women who have to endure such behaviour find it extremely distressing. There are countless numbers of women out there in society living every day in dread of the next time their partner will invade the privacy of their bodies—poking, grabbing, pinching, groping, rubbing, tickling—in a most demeaning way.

Most women who are victims of their partner's sexual harassment, and who talk to a counsellor about it, admit to being confused by it. When they ask their partner to stop, he tells them this type of behaviour is normal between married couples and that, if they don't like it, there must be something wrong with them. Some of the women who talk to me about it in counselling tell me that one of the reasons they are confused is that, on the one hand, they quite like having sex with their partner but, on the other hand, they hate the way he "mauls" them whenever they walk anywhere near him.

> You can't sit down to watch TV without his hands being all over you.

> I'm walking from the stove to the table ready to serve the meal and he puts his hand under me and grabs my genitals from behind.

> I can be stretching up putting books up on the top shelf of the bookshelf, and he comes up behind me and grabs my breasts. It makes me feel so awful. All I want to do is run away and hide.

When a man abuses his wife in this way, she will, for her own protection, devise ways of never being anywhere near him. Also, she will be quickly turned off sex because the love-making she once enjoyed will be a reminder of all the times he has invaded the privacy of her body and made her feel dirty.

Marriage does not mean that your husband owns your body and can do whatever he likes with it.

Your body is your own. You choose to share your body with your partner when you agree to have sex with him but, apart from that, he has no right at all to touch your breasts or genitals. He has no right to touch you sexually without your consent. Most women like to be touched and hugged affectionately but, when a man turns a hug into a "grope", as many men do, it makes a woman feel violated and degraded. Sexual harassment is sexual abuse, and it is wrong!

Most men who do it say they are just wanting to have a bit of fun. They are just teasing and the whole problem is that their partner can't take a joke. Well, it isn't fun for the woman who is the victim of his "teasing". The fact that many of these men refuse to stop their harassment even after their partner tells them it's not fun for her, indicates that there is a lot more to it than playful teasing. It is more like a deliberate act of aggression. It is the way some men choose to express their power over their partner. If she is kept on her toes, worrying about when the groping is going to happen again, if she is constantly demeaned and degraded, then she is rendered powerless. If her mental and emotional energy is taken up focusing on how to avoid his abuse, she is weakened and he has the upper hand.

Suggestions for action

Give his teasing and unwanted touching its correct name—sexual harassment

Sexual harassment is against the law. If you give your partner's behaviour its correct label, it will be easier for you to remind yourself that he is committing a criminal act. Every time he invades your privacy and intrudes upon your private bodily space, he is not indulging in a harmless bit of fun as he would have you believe. He is actually committing a crime of sexual abuse.

Talk to him about how it makes you feel

If your partner abuses you in this way, it may be that he doesn't realise how it is affecting you. Giving him the benefit of the doubt, your first step must be to talk to him about how you feel. If he is genuinely unaware of the effect his behaviour is having and if he genuinely doesn't want to do anything you find unpleasant, he will stop. If he doesn't stop, it will be devastating for you because you will then know that he cares more about his own "fun" than about how you feel.

Put up barriers to protect yourself from his abuse

If you don't want to leave him and are willing to settle for a relationship that is less than satisfactory in some areas, you must erect barriers to protect yourself from his unwanted attacks on your body. A relationship in which one partner is compelled to build barriers against the other is definitely less than satisfactory but, in the long run, the building of such barriers is less damaging than the effect of one partner being constantly abused and degraded by the other.

Strenuously guard your right to privacy

Remember, your body is your own. No one has the right to invade it. Insist that others, including your partner, respect your right to privacy. Women who succeed in protecting their bodies from intrusion and harassment feel stronger because they are more in control of their own lives.

21. When you discover your partner has sexually abused your child

Women who have had the experience of discovering their partner has been sexually abusing their child or children say it is the most disturbing and distressing experience they have ever had. Whether a mother discovers it herself by catching her partner in the act, or the child finds the strength and courage to tell her, or a friend the child has confided in tells her, a mother experiences an incredible jumble of feelings—shock, disbelief, panic, confusion, guilt, anger.

In relation to her child, she feels an overwhelming concern for the child's welfare, fear and panic about how it will affect the child's emotional and psychological development into the future, and guilt that she was not able to protect her child from such criminal abuse.

In relation to her partner, she is in shock and disbelief that he was capable of committing a criminal act of such magnitude, that he was prepared to stoop so low as to put an innocent child's future happiness and stability at risk to satisfy his own need for sexual power and control. Also, she feels incredible anger toward him and a deep sense of betrayal. She trusted him. She trusted her children to his care. And he has betrayed that trust in a most despicable way. How could he do this to her lovely, innocent children? What kind of monster is he that he would deliberately put these children through such trauma—trauma that will scar them to a greater or lesser degree for the rest of their lives?

Children are so vulnerable. When they are born, they depend for their survival on the care of adults. If they are lucky enough to have two loving, sensible, responsible parents, then they have every chance of faring well. Or, if they are lucky enough to have a responsible mother who is a sole parent, committed to bringing up her children without a male partner, they have every chance of faring well. But if one or both parents are irresponsible and self-absorbed, then they are in danger of being used to satisfy their parents' needs.

Studies show that perpetrators of childhood sexual abuse are 99 per cent male. They are fathers, stepfathers, grandfathers, older brothers, uncles, "friends" of the family.

While girls are more often the victims of sexual abuse in the home, boys are also victims. Statistics vary, but most studies reveal that one in four girls is a victim of sexual abuse and one in seven boys.

If you are one of the many mothers who have experienced this particular kind of trauma, that of discovering your child was being sexually abused by your partner, then you would have asked yourself: Why? Why did your partner do such a terrible thing? The explanation most commonly given, and which is wrong, is that a perpetrator of sexual abuse has such a strong sex drive and he simply had to satisfy his urges. Two very convenient conclusions are drawn from such an explanation. One is that the perpetrator couldn't help himself and we ought to feel sorry for him. The other is that his wife is to blame because she mustn't be "giving" him enough sex to satisfy him. If his sexual appetite were satisfied, he wouldn't have to look for it in his children. *Wrong! Wrong! Wrong!*

Sexual abuse has very little to do with sexual needs and everything to do with power needs. A man who sexually assaults children, a man who touches, molests, abuses children, enjoys the power he has over his small and vulnerable victims. Indeed, the power turns him on.

He has total control, and he loves it. He can place a child's hand on his penis and know that she won't dare take her hand away or that, if she does, he can simply put it back there again. He can make her suck his penis. He can ejaculate in her mouth. He can make her take off her clothes. He can make her stand still while he touches her wherever he wants to. He can rape her. She may be crying. She may be protesting. But he knows she will do as he tells her because she is the child and he is the adult. He has total control.

I am sickened when I hear people excuse a perpetrator by saying: "He loves his daughter so much. It just got out of control." I am sickened because, in the same way as sexual abuse is not about sex, it is also not about love. Any act which scars a child for life can never be about love.

A woman who discovers her partner has sexually abused her child has some difficult decisions to make:
1. Should she report his criminal behaviour to the police?
2. Should she leave him?
3. Should she tell his family?
4. Should she tell her own family?
My answers to the above questions are: Yes, Yes, Yes and Yes. Any attempt to protect a perpetrator of sexual abuse is tantamount to condoning his behaviour and, if his behaviour is condoned, it is more likely than not that he will do it again. The only hope for change exists in his admitting his criminal behaviour, being truly sorry (not *pretend* sorry), really wanting to change, and moving out of home for a period of months (away from contact with the victim) during which time he will undergo serious therapy aimed at behaviour-change.

Suggestions for action

Don't ever excuse his behaviour

Sexual abuse of a child is inexcusable. If your partner has betrayed you and your children in this way, whatever you do, don't fall into the trap of looking for excuses for his behaviour. Of course, if you do refuse to excuse and forgive him, there will be those who will call you "hard" and "uncompromising". Your partner, himself, will say to you "I've said I'm sorry. What more do you want me to do?" He will come up with all sorts of excuses, but it is important that you don't accept any of them.

Intellectually-able adults have the capacity to think ahead, to weigh up the consequences of their actions before they act. Your partner has that ability but he chose either to ignore the need to weigh up the consequences of his actions or, having looked at the possible consequences, he made the choice to go ahead anyhow. Like a self-centred child, the impulse to satisfy his own wants and needs was greater than his desire to do the right thing. Such behaviour can never be excused or forgiven.

Don't ever accept the blame

There will be those who will blame you. A mother is always a convenient target when relatives, the church, the police and others in the community are looking for someone to blame. I wonder why people find it so hard to blame the one who actually committed the crime. They say things like: "The child's mother must have known it was happening." Or "It was easier for the mother to turn a blind eye to what was happening to her daughter than to have to satisfy her partner's sexual needs herself." Or "If she'd had sex every time he wanted it, he wouldn't have had to turn to the children."

These are stupid, ignorant comments made by people who are too afraid to place the blame where it belongs. In a society where men set themselves up as the foundation on which everything is built and the security on which everyone must depend, it is scary to admit that so many men bash their wives and molest their children. What would happen if we placed the blame for these kinds of crimes where it actually belongs? What would happen if we blamed men? Nobody knows, and most people are afraid to find out. At the very least, we would have to admit that the foundation on which our society is built has huge cracks in it and our security as a community of people is in jeopardy. It's much easier, therefore, to blame the mother. She already feels guilt about not having been aware enough to protect her child from the abuse, so she is an easy target. Put the blame on her and she will probably accept it. Then, as a society, we can go on covering up the truth and wondering why our precious children continue to be raped and abused.

If you are in this situation, you can begin turning things around. To put pressure on your partner to change, all you have to do, initially, is refuse to accept the blame for his criminal behaviour. You are not guilty. He is. If you refuse to accept the blame, he may have to.

Contact the police

This is a criminal offence and ought to be reported. I know that's difficult but, even if you decide in a couple of weeks not to pursue charges against your partner, contacting the police gives him the message that he has committed a serious offence and that you are not willing to treat it lightly.

Leave him

If you can see your way clear to leave him, you really ought to. He has betrayed your child in a most fundamental way. And, in doing that, he has betrayed you as well. The one thing you know is that you'll never be able to trust him again. You thought you knew him but now everything has been thrown into chaos. It's like being married to a stranger, an evil stranger. Leave him if you can but, if you can't, then make a resolve to be very vigilant in the future.

Don't ever leave your children alone with him again

Many women in this situation feel that they ought to forgive their partner and, as a sign of that forgiveness, force themselves to trust him as completely as they did before. And when such women catch themselves worrying about whether their children really are safe with him, whether he really is trustworthy, they feel guilty and berate themselves for not having enough trust. I want to say to you as strongly as I can: Don't trust him! You are right to worry. If he were trustworthy around children, he would never have sexually abused them in the first place. Even if he has had some visits to a counsellor and tells you he is "cured", don't trust him. The sexual abuse of children is not a sickness. It is a crime. It is not sick behaviour which can be cured. It is criminal behaviour which requires punishment, followed by a total transformation.

Some women experience a dilemma with regard to leaving their partner once they discover he has been sexually abusing one or more of their children. The dilemma for women springs from the legal requirement that, when parents are separated or divorced, both parents must have access to the children. It is said to be "in the best interests of the child". Many concerned mothers reason that if they stay in the marriage till the children are teenagers, they will have more chance of controlling the kinds of contact the father has with the children. If she is on hand, a woman reasons, there will be more chance of her being able to manipulate situations so that the children are never left in his care. What a terrible way to have to live! But I can see how that situation would be infinitely better for a mother than having to hand over her vulnerable children on a regular basis to the one who has abused them. In the case of separation or divorce, that is exactly what the law would require. Mothers who refuse to obey the law, of course, are in danger of having their children taken off them and given to the perpetrator on a full-time basis. Remember, all of this is said to be "for the good of the child".

There is some movement among women's groups in Western countries to have the law changed so that parents who commit crimes of sexual abuse against children and, indeed, any crimes of violence in the home which impact upon children, will be disqualified from any further contact with those children. The violence itself, the sexual abuse itself, would be enough to prove that future contact with that parent would *not* be "in the best interests of the child". While women's groups will continue to push for justice in these terms, we acknowledge that the law in Western countries was developed by men, is administered mainly by men, and exists for the benefit of middle- and upper-class men, and that change, therefore, will be a long time coming.

Till the law in relation to families is changed to reflect justice for women and children, women must make their own decisions to leave or not to leave based on what they decide will be best for themselves as well as their children.

22. When no one believes you

Men who sexually abuse their children are usually very careful to cover all their tracks, making it almost impossible to discover what they are doing. Also, many of them give the impression that they are good fathers, devoted to their children. Your friends and relatives sometimes comment to you on how lucky you are to have a partner who spends so much time with the children. That's what you think, too, until the truth comes out.

As hard as it is for you to believe, it is sometimes even harder for friends and relatives to believe. The experience of some women is that when they most needed the support of those closest to them, all they received was condemnation. They were accused of lying. Nobody believed them. In fact, it was their partner who received the support and comfort because he was being "wrongly accused" by a "vindictive woman".

Suggestions for action

Believe in yourself and what you know

If you have evidence that your partner has sexually abused your child, don't waver in terms of what you know. Believe in yourself. If you suspect your partner is sexually abusing your child but are not sure, look for proof so that you can be sure.

It does happen, on rare occasions, that mothers who suspect abuse is occurring are wrong but, instead of putting your suspicions aside and doing nothing (for fear of being wrong), it is crucial that you pay attention to, and act on, your suspicions. Confront your partner and, if he denies it and you are still not convinced, begin an investigation of your own.

Believe your child

Sometimes the only "proof" you have is that your child told you it happened. This is proof enough.

Talk to someone who will believe you

This is an extremely traumatic time in your life and, when friends and relatives refuse to believe you, it can also be a very lonely time. Go to a Women's Centre or a Sexual Assault Service and speak to a counsellor. They are trained to deal specifically with these kinds of situations and most are very skilled at what they do. If you just want to talk about it and have someone listen to how you feel, tell them that. The fact that you go to talk to someone at a Sexual Assault Service doesn't mean you have to take it further and get the police involved. A counsellor's role is to listen and to keep confidentiality. If you decide to contact police, the counsellor's role is to support you and be there for you. If you prefer a more private setting, then make an appointment to see a counsellor in private practice. You do need to talk. And you do need to know that the person you are talking to believes you.

23. Discovering your partner's stash of pornography

Whenever the issue of the rights and wrongs of pornography comes up for discussion, there are usually three distinct opinions. One is that all pornography is harmless and that a man who likes to "perv" at naked and semi-naked women in magazines, on videos or on the internet, a man who indulges his fantasies in phone sex, is not hurting anyone. Another opinion is that some pornography is all right and some should be banned. Those who hold this view use the label "erotica" instead of "pornography" and make a distinction between violent and non-violent erotica. Violent erotica, that is, pornography produced for the consumption of those men who get turned on by violence against women and children, is not acceptable, they say, while non-violent erotica is acceptable. A third opinion, and the one I subscribe to passionately, is that all pornography is harmful and should, therefore, be banned.

Lots of women tell me they have a gut reaction against pornography but can't explain why they feel that way. Maybe it will help if I give my own reasons for believing pornography is harmful:

• *Pornography, or so-called "erotic" material, exploits and degrades the women and children actually photographed.* Most people seem to agree that pornography involving children is unacceptable, but the suggestion that pornography involving women is exploitative of women is hotly contested. The "freedom of speech and expression" argument, which is very popular and always used, maintains that if the "models" pose willingly and if they get paid well for the work, there is no exploitation and any attempt to ban pornography would result in depriving women of work. It is true that many women do this work willingly. They see it as a job and get paid for what they do. It is not unlike prostitution in that regard. Many prostitutes decide to work in the sex industry because it appears to be an easy way to earn a living. But that doesn't alter the fact that those women and children who work in prostitution and/or pornography are being exploited to satisfy the needs of men who get pleasure out of using others in this depersonalised and detached way.

- *Pornography exploits and degrades all women and, consequently, the whole of society is the poorer.* When the female body is objectified and depersonalised and reduced to those parts which turn men on, when the female body is used by men as an object of fantasy for the purpose of masturbation and sexual release, all women are degraded. All women are reduced to the status of objects for men's sexual gratification. The truth is that women are much more than their sexual parts but men who use pornography refuse to acknowledge that. As I see it, it is the right of all women to be acknowledged and responded to as human beings with equal rights to men, equally worthy of being treated with respect and dignity.

- *Pornography creates a society in which it is acceptable for one half of the population to be exploited and degraded for the pleasure of the other.* With the existence of pornography, men's freedom to indulge themselves becomes women's lack of freedom to be treated with respect and dignity.

- *Pornography creates a situation, at a personal level, where individual women find themselves being used as depositories in which their partners "relieve themselves" after having been turned on by depersonalised images of female body parts.* Such a situation is damaging to women and extremely destructive of relationships. This is not the way most women imagined their sexual relationship with their partner would be. They imagined it would be a warm, loving, intimate, exciting experience—a shared experience of love and sexual pleasure. Instead, a woman whose partner indulges in pornography finds that he has already had his excitement with a photograph or video of a total stranger, before approaching her. When he does approach her, it is to relieve himself or, as someone once described to me crudely, but honestly, "to empty his dirty water".

- *Pornography encourages men to use their partners for sexual experimentation.* When this happens, women are used as guinea pigs. Sex, which is hailed as an expression of love and commitment between two people, is turned into an experiment. Men experiment on their partners by imitating the degrading positions and acts they have seen on videos and in magazines.

So, what do you do if you discover your partner is into pornography, either on a regular basis or only occasionally? As discussed above, most women have an immediate negative reaction to such a discovery. They don't like it. They may not understand why they feel that way but the thought of the man they love and share an intimate sexual relationship with "drooling" over images of the naked bodies of other women (and children) makes them feel sick. The thought of him masturbating at the sound of a woman's voice talking dirty on one of those phone sex lines, makes them want to throw up.

When women confront their partners about their discovery, they are commonly told to "grow up" or to "stop being a prude" or that "all men do it" or that "it doesn't mean anything". Many women are confused by their own strong reaction against it. What if their partner is right? they ask themselves. What if it is true that the use of pornography is a harmless activity indulged in by lots of men and that their reaction does indicate that they are prudish? Maybe they should try to change their attitude. And so, they try. They work at being open-minded about it. But still, it doesn't feel right to them— probably for the reasons discussed above. Pornography does demean women and children. It destroys relationships. It creates a society made up of the users and the used. And it encourages us all to condone and support a culture of exploitation. I, for one, will not do that.

Suggestions for action

Don't try to force yourself to accept it

When you discover your partner uses pornography, take notice of how it makes you feel. If you hate it and wish he would stop, don't think of yourself as a "prude" or "old-fashioned". Rather, be proud of yourself that you wish for something better for your relationship and your society. Be pleased that you are not persuaded by the arguments of the pornography industry and its supporters. Remember that, in refusing to condone the exploiting, the degrading, the demeaning of women and children in this way, you are making a contribution toward the development of a healthier, happier, less abusive society.

Since you don't condone pornography, don't pretend that you do. Don't try to make yourself accept your partner's use of it. Be straight with him about what you think and feel.

Talk to your partner about how you feel

Communication is always the key to resolving an issue of disagreement in any relationship. As soon as a woman discovers her partner's interest in pornographic magazines or videos or phone sex, she ought to talk to him and tell him how she feels. Remember, though, that whenever you disagree with an immature man's point of view about anything, he will more than likely interpret that as personal criticism and respond by being defensive. Whenever he puts up his shield to defend himself, be prepared for the fact that a fair and rational discussion is not going to take place. Still, you can try.

24. When he refuses to discuss it

When pornography comes between two people in a relationship, it usually proves to be a very difficult issue to resolve because a compromise is hardly possible. When a man sees nothing wrong with using pornography and his partner feels exploited and cheapened by his use of it, it's not as if the two of them can negotiate and agree to meet halfway. "I'll cut down on my use of pornography if you try to be a bit more accepting." No. It's one of those issues where compromise doesn't work because, if a man indulges in a little bit of pornography instead of a lot, he is still using pornography and his partner still feels degraded and demeaned.

It is important that you confront your partner as soon as you discover that he uses pornography and tell him how it makes you feel. Some women have found that when they took the time to explain their feelings, their partner admitted that the pornography he used from time to time wasn't important to him. He just did it out of curiosity. And now that he knew how it upset his partner, he would stop immediately. I hope it's like that for you but, to be honest, I must say that most women find it much more difficult than that. Many men who are consumers of pornography develop a kind of addiction to it. In these cases, the sexual pleasure experienced through fantasy and masturbation, with the help of pornographic material, becomes more exciting to them than any other form of sexual activity.

If the man you are living with lacks emotional maturity, he will take your attempt to discuss your feelings about the issue as a direct personal insult. He will respond by being defensive, and he will defend himself either by verbally attacking you or by withdrawing. In either case, there will be no attempt to discuss it, no attempt to listen to how you feel. He will already have made up his mind. He is right and you are wrong. He is open-minded about these things and you are closed-minded. He is an adult and you need to grow up.

If his defence is to attack, he will not be interested in entering into an equal discussion. Rather, he will set about telling you why you should agree with him that pornography is harmless. He will tell you you are just being silly. He will presume you are jealous. He will attempt to reassure you by telling you that you are more important to him, you are more sexy, you turn him on more than any of the pornographic material he uses. But, when you suggest he, therefore, stop using it, he will refuse. He will insist that you have no right to tell him what to do. "It's a free country. I'll do what I like."

The more you try to explain how you feel, the more determined he will become. The more you try to explain that it is not a matter of simple jealousy but the much larger issue of his attitude toward women in general, the more abusive he will become. He won't listen. He won't want to hear you express your concern about his getting pleasure out of exploiting and dissecting and using women in this way.

If his defence is to withdraw rather than to attack, the result in terms of communication will be similar. While the man who defends his behaviour by attacking will speak and not listen, the man who defends his behaviour by withdrawing will neither speak nor listen. In both instances, no communication occurs.

Suggestions for action

When a man decides there is to be no discussion about his use of pornography, a woman is left to deal with her thoughts and feelings by herself. As in other similar situations, her options are: to leave him; to close her mind to her own opinions and feelings and accept his use of pornography as his right; or to withdraw emotionally and sexually, remaining in the relationship only in a partial kind of way.

Can't live with him,

can't live without him

25. When you suspect your partner is having an affair

Men and women who have affairs, that is, sexual relationships or sexual liaisons with others while still being in a committed relationship, are indulging in harmful acts of betrayal. What is it that constitutes betrayal in these situations? Is it having sex with someone who is not your spouse? No. Is it developing an emotional relationship with someone who is not your spouse? No. Then, what is it? *It is doing those things when you promised you would not.* Any commitment entered into by two people, whether by formal marriage or not, usually implies a promise to be faithful. It is the breaking of that promise that constitutes betrayal. *And it is all the lies you tell to make sure your deceit is covered up.*

People who have affairs usually justify their unfaithfulness by arguing that there is nothing wrong with having sex with more than one partner. Everybody's doing it, they say. But the truth is everybody is *not* doing it. Many people believe that a promise is a promise, that a commitment is there to be honoured and that any act of betrayal is, also, a betrayal of oneself.

If there is nothing wrong with having sex and/or developing a relationship with someone outside one's primary relationship, one wonders why so many people go to such lengths to hide the fact that they are having affairs. If you are one of those women who suspects her partner is having an affair but can't find any real proof, rest assured that it is not because you walk around with your eyes closed. The truth is that most men go to a lot of trouble to cover their tracks, to make sure their partner never finds out. Some even enlist the support of their mates to cover for them, to lie for them, if ever the need arises.

One of the hardest things for women to deal with after they discover their partner has, indeed, been having an affair is the humiliation of knowing they have been taken for a fool for the entire time the affair has been going on. So, if you suspect your partner is being unfaithful and would really like to save yourself this embarrassment, look for tell-tale signs. Here are some of them:

- *A lessening interest, or a total loss of interest, in sex.* Some women are pleased when their partner becomes less demanding about sex while others are quite distressed by it and agonise over what could have happened to cause their partner to "lose his sex drive".

- *Changes in the time he spends away from home.* He begins staying at work later and later. Or he finds reasons why he has to go early to football practice. Or he suddenly insists on driving the kids to ballet lessons or soccer practice on weekends, when it had fallen to you to drive them everywhere for the past ten years.

- *Changes in his appearance.* A man who is having an affair often tries to look younger or sexier or more fashionable than he used to. He begins to take more interest in his clothes. Many start wearing jewellery (gold chains, rings) for the first time in their lives.

- *Changes in personality.* Some men become much more alive and interesting when they start having an affair. They change from being dull and boring to animated and witty, laughing and joking like excited little boys. Others become depressed and withdrawn, causing their partners to worry about what could be wrong. Most women believe that when a person is consistently depressed, it is a sensible move to go and talk to a doctor or counsellor to try to get it worked out. No amount of urging, of course, will get a man who is having an affair to agree to seek help for his depression because he already knows what's wrong with him. It is only his wife/partner who doesn't know and she is deliberately kept in the dark and left to worry.

Most women are taken by surprise when they find themselves entertaining thoughts about whether or not their partner could be having an affair. At first, they dismiss their suspicions out of hand because the idea of it seems ludicrous. It is when the suspicions keep coming back that one needs to begin to take one's thoughts a little more seriously.

If you have ever suspected your partner was having an affair, you'll know that to suspect can be almost as hard as actually knowing. A nagging suspicion, without any confirmation that the situation you suspect actually exists, can cause serious anxiety.

There are two types of anxiety—normal and abnormal. Normal anxiety is that which most people experience when they have to do something stressful, like going to talk to the school principal when your child is about to be suspended, or turning up at work on your first day in a new job. Abnormal anxiety, on the other hand, is anxiety about something which may not exist. It is fear welling up inside you for which there is no apparent cause.

In addition to anxiety and fear, you can also feel guilt. To find yourself having thoughts about whether or not you can trust this man you love causes you to feel really guilty. You have no proof that he is cheating on you. You only have your own nagging thoughts. You feel disloyal and guilty, and you also feel paranoid. "Maybe I'm making it all up. Maybe my imagination is getting away from me. Maybe I'm having some kind of breakdown."

When you have persistent suspicions that your partner may be having an affair, the best thing to do is take your suspicions seriously. It isn't helpful when a friend or relative you have confided in tells you you're imagining it and that the best thing to do is to ignore your suspicions. That isn't very helpful advice because you know you have already tried ignoring them, but they persist. You can't ignore something that refuses to be ignored. You have to accept your thoughts, take them seriously and figure out a way to act on them.

Suggestions for action

Ask your partner

When you have suspicions that won't go away, it is best to confront the issue head-on. But, whatever you do, don't launch into a whole lot of accusations. When men feel insecure about their relationships, for whatever reason, it is quite common for them to launch into serious and degrading accusations. "You're a slut." "Who are you having it off with this week?" If a man really wants to know, hurtful accusations are not the way to go. And the same is true for you.

Simply tell your partner how you are feeling. Tell him you've been having these thoughts about whether or not he is involved with someone else. Tell him what you have experienced about his behaviour: that he seems to be distracted, seems to have his mind on something else most of the time; or that he seems to look for any excuse to be away from home. Ask him to be honest with you because, if he is having an affair, you would rather know.

A mature man will realise you have a right to ask and, indeed, that you ought to ask so as to settle the questions in your mind and relieve your concerns. The two of you would, then, discuss changes that could be made (in his style of communicating, perhaps) that would prevent your fears building up again. This is the best outcome and one which would result in strengthening your relationship in the long-term.

Most times, however, when women raise the question about whether or not their partner is having an affair, the discussion which follows is not easy. Also, no matter what form the discussion takes, there is no guarantee that, at the end of the discussion, you will have found out what you wanted to know. But don't be put off. The only fair thing to do, before taking any other action, is to ask him and give him the chance to explain. He will respond in one of the following ways:

- *Calm and logical.* If your partner prides himself on being logical, he will be calm and will present you with a perfectly logical explanation which you will be expected to accept. A logical explanation does not always mean it is a truthful explanation but, if something sounds logical, you will more than likely accept it—until your suspicions begin to rise again.

- *Hurt and indignant.* If your partner is not having an affair, he could respond to your question by being hurt and disappointed and indignant. This is a difficult response to deal with because your aim is not to hurt him but, rather, to settle your own fears. The difficulty is that, when there is no way to settle your fears but to confront the situation head-on, you have to do it and hope he recovers quickly from the hurt. If your partner *is* having an affair, he could still respond by being hurt and disappointed and indignant. Men who set out to deceive can be good actors. They can act "deeply hurt". They can even add a tear or two to make you feel really bad. They can be so convincing as to have you apologising for

ever doubting their faithfulness and apologising for
the hurt you've caused.

- *Sullen and withdrawn.* If your partner is sometimes
moody, your question could send him into a bad one!
As is always the case with people who withdraw as a
way of avoiding communication, you will not know
what his sullenness means. Has he withdrawn
because he's not guilty and is hurt by your doubts
about his faithfulness, or has he withdrawn because
he is guilty and refuses to confirm or deny it?

- *Angry and abusive.* If your partner is someone who
gets angry and abusive, any question about his faithfulness could set him off, so be prepared. Whether he
is guilty or not, he will become defensive, and attack
will be his method of defence. Most probably, he will
turn on you and accuse you of "sleeping around".
He will attempt to shift the focus on to the question
of *your* fidelity so that he can gain the upper hand.
It's important not to allow yourself to be rail-roaded
by his bullying and intimidation. As far as possible,
keep the focus on the original question which was a
question about *his* fidelity.

Whether his response is calm and logical, hurt and indignant, sullen and withdrawn, or angry and abusive, the
answer to your question will still probably not be clear. Is
he having an affair or not? To attempt to discuss your
fears, however, is an important first step. It may be, after
you have raised the issue with him, that you feel
reassured and your fears have settled down. If so, leave it
there and get on with enjoying your relationship.

*Allow for the possibility that your suspicions
could be wrong*

Even if your fears don't settle down and your suspicions
continue, it is advisable to keep in mind that you could

be wrong. When your suspicions persist, you must take them seriously and begin to look for proof, but always allow for the possibility that you could be wrong.

Look for proof

If your fears do not settle down after confronting your partner and getting his response, you must begin looking for proof (see Situation 10). Even though, if he has broken his commitment, you would rather not have to confront it, it is better for you to know than to spend your years anxiously wondering. Think of it like this: the decision to begin looking for proof is a decision to take control of your own anxieties. If you don't find any proof, then relax and enjoy your relationship. If you do, then remember, you needed to know. Every woman has the right to know if her partner has secretly changed the rules of the agreement by which she is still living. Once you know you are being lied to and deceived, you are free to live by the new rules. I'm not recommending that you, also, go out and have an affair but, at least, you are free to begin making plans for your future which may or may not include your present partner.

Look for tell-tale signs

When you decide to look for proof, the easiest way to start is to open your eyes and look for any of the tell-tale signs mentioned above. It's surprising how easy it is to go about our daily routine and just not see changes in our partner's appearance or behaviour, even when they are staring us in the face. While the presence or absence of any such sign doesn't, in itself, amount to proof of anything, it is always a good place to start.

26. When you discover your partner is having an affair

Many women who speak to me about suspecting their partner is having an affair tell me that they wouldn't feel right embarking on a search for proof. "It doesn't seem fair," they say. Or "I wouldn't like to pry." Why? If your suspicions are causing you to be anxious or depressed, or if you are suffering insomnia because of your fears, you must do something. Also, when it's a question of whether or not your partner has broken your agreement without telling you, it could be that your insistence on "fairness" is pretty one-sided.

When your suspicions are found to be true, that is, when you actually discover your partner is involved with someone else, you will be devastated. A whole mixture of feelings will well up inside you all at once—shock, hurt, humiliation, anger, a deep sense of loss. The feelings of loss you experience are as bad as, if not worse than, they would be if he had died or walked out on you. Some men do decide to leave once their secret is out in the open, but most insist that they want to stay. The relationship he has with *you* is the important one in his life, he may say. The other is just "a bit on the side". In those circumstances, you haven't actually lost him because he is still with you, but the sense of loss you experience is real and unmistakable.

If you haven't lost him, then what is this deep sense of loss you feel deep down inside yourself? What is this grieving? The fact is you *have* lost the man you loved. The man living with you now is someone quite different from the man you thought you shared a commitment with. You are grieving for the loss of truth, loyalty, certainty. No matter what the future holds, whether you stay together or part company, you sense it will never be the same again. What you had together is lost forever. Your dreams of growing old together in peace and serenity are gone. You may still grow old together, but your dreams have been shattered and you can only hope that new dreams will develop in their place.

You remember how patient you were while all the time he was living a lie and surreptitiously entangling you in it. You think of the number of times you gave him the benefit of the doubt by interpreting his behaviour in a way that was supportive of him. When he seemed to be avoiding sex and other intimacies, you put it down to the fact that he was tired from working too hard. Now you know it was because he was getting all the sex he wanted from his lover. When he was so often withdrawn and uncommunicative, you worried about how stressed he must be. You kept the children from annoying him because he needed peace and quiet, he needed space. Now you know it was because he was thinking of her. When he seemed sad and depressed, you urged him to go to a doctor but he wouldn't. You worried that he might be sick, or that he was concerned about his work, or his earning capacity, or growing older, or 101 other possibilities. He wouldn't talk about what was depressing him so you were left to ponder and worry and feel anxious all by yourself. Now you know it was simply because he wanted to be with her or because he was worrying about being found out.

What a waste of your precious time and energy! He knew you were worrying about him, caring about his well-being, doing everything you could to help him feel better, and he let you go on doing that while he continued to lie and deceive you. Now, you look back and think of all the things you said and did out of caring, and wonder how many laughs he and his lover had at your expense. This is major betrayal!

To this point, I have discussed the situation of a woman discovering that her husband is having an affair with another woman. But what if the person he is having an affair with is a man? In recent years, it has become clear that such a situation is much more commonplace than we ever realised. The fact is that many men with homosexual tendencies work hard, particularly in their younger years, at denying their sexual interest in other men. They know what they feel but, because of society's ongoing discrimination against gay men, they refuse (either consciously or unconsciously) to allow themselves to pursue the lifestyle that feels natural and right for them. They do what everyone else seems to be doing. They meet a woman, fall in love, get married and have children. Many of these men who discuss their situation later on in life admit that their homosexual desire, their desire for other men, has never diminished. Some choose not to act on that desire, preferring to remain sexually faithful to their wives. Others either seek casual sex with men or enter into short- or long-term homosexual relationships.

Some women, on discovering their partner's interest in other men, seem to be able to rationalise that some people are naturally bisexual and, after setting a few rules about safe sex, proceed on the understanding that their partner will, from time to time, have sex with men. Most women, on the other hand, cannot and will not accept it. Whether one's partner is having an affair (or a series of one-night stands) with a man or a woman, it is still experienced as betrayal.

What should you do when you discover your partner is having an affair, or indulging in one-night stands, or buying the services of a prostitute? There is no set plan of action, no one plan of action to suit all situations, but the one thing that is recommended in all cases is that you confront him about it. Don't keep your discovery to yourself. Some women seem to reason that if they pretend it isn't happening or if they don't make an issue of it, it may go away. For your own emotional and psychological well-being, it is crucial that you face the reality of your situation. If you have proof that your partner is involved with someone else, talk to him about it. To cover it up is to collude with him in his deceit. Tell him that you know. He may object. He may deny it. He may get angry. None of that matters as much as your determination to live a life ruled by truth rather than lies.

Confronting your partner about it, though, will not be easy. Lots of women say: "If I ever found out my husband was having an affair, I'd pack his bags and send him on his way." It's easy to be brave and definite about what one would do when speaking hypothetically. But when one is faced with a real situation, it is never as easy. Some women have confided in me that once they had proof that their partner was having an affair, they were really fearful about confronting him. They didn't want to ignore it and pretend it wasn't happening, but the thought of talking about it made them very anxious. Other women have said that they had no fear at all. They were so angry at what they had discovered that their anger gave them plenty of strength and courage for the confrontation.

If you are one of those women who are fearful about the confrontation or conversation you are about to initiate, it is important to look at your fears. What is it that makes you afraid?

- It could be that you are afraid of finally putting what you have suspected for some time into words. That which is unspoken seems, somehow, less real than that which is spoken. Words have a way of making something unavoidably real, and that's frightening.

- It could be that you are afraid your partner will deny it even in the face of the proof you present. If he does deny it, it makes any hope of an ultimate resolution of the problem an impossibility. In presenting it to him for discussion, you are offering him the chance to talk about the agreement which formed the basis of your relationship originally, with a view to coming to a different agreement if that's what he wants. But if he begins by denying what you know to be the truth, then there seems little hope for honest communication.

- It could be that you are afraid your partner will take your confrontation as an opportunity to tell you he is leaving you.

- It could be that you are afraid you'll never be happy again. You have no way of knowing what will happen once it's out in the open, being talked about and cried about and agonised over. All you know is, it feels like you are more distressed and unhappy at this moment than you have ever been before, and you can't bear the thought of that unhappiness deepening. When you try to look into the future, all you can see is unhappiness and despair, and your fear almost immobilises you.

But you *must* go ahead and talk to him about your discovery. You have to be strong enough in your mind to overcome your fears and know that confronting the situation, right now, will be much better for you (and, indeed, for everyone else concerned) in the long-term.

While bringing it up for discussion is a must, everything else you do is up to you. You may decide to leave him. You may decide to seek counselling. You may decide to stay with him on the understanding that he break all contact with the other person. You may decide to do nothing except keep yourself and the children surviving from day to day. Whatever action you decide to take must be your own action. By all means, talk to friends and relatives, talk to a counsellor, because you will need emotional support, but make your own decisions.

Suggestions for action

Confront your partner about your discovery

This has already been thoroughly discussed above. I mention it here again as a reminder of how crucial it is.

Don't blame yourself

The first impulse most women have when something bad happens is to blame themselves (see Situation 36). Let me stress that, when you *have* done something wrong or hurtful to someone else, when you *are* blameworthy, then you ought to blame yourself. But when your partner is the one who has broken the commitment you shared, when he is the one who is guilty, there is absolutely nothing to be gained from blaming yourself. All that does is give your partner an excuse to feel that he is not guilty and add to the injustice that already exists.

A common argument many women subscribe to goes like this: "It must be my fault. I must have been doing something wrong. Otherwise, he wouldn't have looked for love or sex with someone else." That kind of thinking doesn't make a lot of sense. A man who decides to get involved with another woman (or man) will do it regardless of how good a partner you have been.

Don't blame the other woman

Of course, there is some blame attributable to the other woman but she is not to blame in any major way, and she is certainly not to blame exclusively. If she knew he was married or in a committed relationship, she is guilty of knowingly becoming involved with a man who already had a commitment to his partner. But that is all. Some women in their desperate attempts to figure out why their partner betrayed them so badly, settle on the idea that he was just a poor, innocent man, ensnared by this horrible woman who set her sights on him and, finally, caught him unawares. His only fault was that he was too naïve to know what was happening until it was too late. As comforting as it might be to believe such a scenario, it is actually nonsense.

If your partner has become sexually and/or emotionally involved with another woman, it is your partner (not the other woman) who has betrayed you. It is your partner (not the other woman) who has broken the commitment he had with you. It is your partner (not the other woman) who is guilty and who must be held accountable for his actions. Be sure to place the blame where it belongs because that will give you the best chance of working through the hurt, the despair, the anger that you feel.

Don't blame the other man

If it is a *man* your partner is involved with, again there is some blame attributable to him in terms of his becoming involved with someone who he knew was already in a committed relationship, but that is all. It is your partner who has betrayed you and your partner who is to be held accountable for that betrayal.

When a man is secretly involved in homosexual liaisons while being careful to maintain the image of a loving husband and father, there is an added cause for concern which must be considered by his wife once she discovers his secret life. Not only has he deliberately deceived *her* by keeping from her the extent of his sexual interests, but he has also worked hard at deceiving himself. By being careful to present a "respectable" front, he has been able to continue lying to himself about his sexual orientation and to use his wife and children, without their knowledge, to perpetuate his lie.

This is not to say he has lied about the love he feels for his wife or even about his enjoyment of sex with her but that, in keeping his secret from her, he has set up a situation in which he could continue to lie to himself about the importance of his desire for other men. A woman in this kind of situation feels deceived and betrayed, not only by her partner's unfaithfulness but also by the knowledge that he has been lying to himself and, at the same time, using her to support his lie.

If this is your situation, it is important to understand the implications of your partner's deceit and to lay the blame where it belongs. If he had been honest with you from the start, if he had talked with you about his feelings and desires, you would have been in a position to make a decision about whether or not you wanted to enter into a committed relationship on the terms he was offering.

Don't "forgive" your partner too soon, if at all

When you discover your partner is having an affair and confront him with it, he will most probably want you to say you forgive him. Don't say it until you mean it. Contrary to popular belief, you don't *have* to forgive him (see Situation 37). Don't say the words simply because you know that's what he wants to hear or because you believe that's what you ought to do. Forgiveness is something that happens in your heart and mind and only *you* know when you are ready to say the words. Don't be bullied into it or shamed into it. You may *never* feel ready to forgive him and that's acceptable too. At some stage, though, you must be ready to let go of all the negative feelings you have so that you will be free to grow again, but that doesn't have to mean forgiving him.

Attend to your own survival needs

Whenever a person suffers shock and experiences the terrible feelings associated with loss, the only thing to do in the beginning is to "hang on". There is nothing you have to do but survive from day to day. Don't push yourself to do anything else. Be aware that the discovery of your partner's infidelity and betrayal has caused you pain and fear and despair. In the first few weeks, all you have to be concerned about is getting through each day. Focus on survival issues like food and drink and staying healthy. Make sure you continue cooking nutritious meals for yourself and your children. Stay away from alcohol and non-prescription drugs. Pay attention to your physical fitness. Focus on exercising, walking, swimming, going to the gym—whatever you can do to keep yourself fit.

It is important to remember that, whenever you feel swamped by emotional pain and trauma at any time throughout your life, a focus on your physical needs, a focus on your survival in terms of health and fitness, will get you through the worst of it. Then, when you feel able to deal with your emotions and when you feel ready to begin looking at your options for the future, you will.

27. Realising you have been surrounded by lies and deceit for a long time

One of the most devastating aspects of discovering your partner has been having an affair is the realisation that you have been surrounded by lies and deceit for as long as the affair has been going on. For some women, that means weeks or months of their lives are thrown into question. For others, it means years. How does one come to terms with the discovery that one's marriage has been a sham for ten, twenty, thirty years or more? And how is it possible to untangle the truth from the lies?

A woman who discovers her partner has been involved with another woman can become totally preoccupied with trying to sort out the truth from the lies.

> I wonder where he really went that New Year's Eve (fifteen years ago) when he said his mate had had an accident and needed him urgently . . .

> Where was he those times I phoned him at work and nobody could locate him?

> Did he really take that adult education course which supposedly lasted a whole year?

She thinks back on all the incidents that seemed a little strange and all the "explanations" that didn't quite satisfy. She remembers wondering, on more than one occasion, why he was being so evasive and what he was attempting to cover up. But, each time, she let it go. She told herself not to be paranoid and simply got on with life.

Now that you have discovered your partner's infidelity, now that the truth is out and the nagging questions about his evasiveness have been answered, it's as though one puzzle has been replaced by another. Instead of asking yourself "Why is he being so evasive?", you now ask yourself "Why did he do it?" Why did he decide to pursue this line of behaviour when, if he had given any thought at all to your feelings, he would have known he was setting out on a path which had the potential to destroy you? As it happens, you are not destroyed but, at times, you feel very close to it.

When you think about the number of lies and the extent of the deceit, you are overwhelmed by the magnitude of his betrayal. You realise there must have been many, many times when this man you loved and trusted was totally preoccupied with thoughts of how to betray you, what lies to tell, how to act so as to allay any suspicions you may have had. And when you think about the betrayal, you feel humiliated, foolish, stripped of all dignity. That he was prepared to share intimacies with someone else while remaining in a relationship with you, makes you feel exposed and exploited. How much of your private and personal life, how many of your personal discussions and disagreements did he share with her? That he was prepared to take you for a fool, to deceive you over such a long period of time, to demonstrate such a lack of respect, has the effect of robbing you of your sense of dignity and worth. All you know is that you feel awful. There is no peace from the nagging questions: Why did he do it? What did this mean? What did that mean? Does he love me at all? Has he ever loved me? Can I ever believe anything he says? How can I ever know, in the future, if he's telling the truth?

Suggestions for action

Believe in yourself

On those occasions in our lives when everything we depended on for our security seems to be crumbling, when we don't know who we can believe or who to trust, it is crucial to remember that the one person who remains rock solid for us is ourselves. Believe in yourself. When it seems as if everyone else is letting you down, be true to yourself. Keep reminding yourself that you are a worthwhile person, that you have done nothing to deserve this trauma and that, if you continue to believe in yourself, the terrible feelings will pass. Believing in yourself will get you through. It won't take away the pain but it will give you the strength to get through.

Don't become obsessed with the need to think through incidents from the past and expose the lies

You *will* do this, of course. In your quest for the truth, you will go back over the past. You will recall those times when your partner's explanations left you puzzled. You will question him, interrogate him, in your compulsion to find the truth. There is nothing wrong with that. You have a need to know, so you must ask.

Some men, partly because of their need to demonstrate that they are doing "penance" and partly because they genuinely want to help their partner deal with her pain, invite their partner to ask questions whenever she wants to. And women do. For days and weeks and months and years, they ask questions. They go back over the same questions again and again because, the truth is, no explanation ever satisfies the deep despair they feel in their hearts.

What we know about men who genuinely and caringly invite their partners to ask questions whenever they want to, however, is that most of them seem to tire of it fairly quickly. Even after only a few weeks, some men are saying: "Not again! Aren't you over that yet? I said I was sorry. How much longer are you going to punish me?" They have no idea of the depth of their partner's pain and the extent of her need to know.

It is important that you keep asking questions for as long as you need to. All I am suggesting here is that you try to be aware of when your focus on his betrayal is becoming obsessive. It is not good for you to allow your obsessiveness to take control. If, after several months, you find yourself still unable to think about anything else and, if you find yourself compelled to discuss the betrayal every time you have a moment alone with your partner, it would be advisable to begin labelling your behaviour as obsessive. In that way, you will signal to yourself that your compulsion to talk about it has become problematic.

When allowed free rein, obsessive thoughts and behaviour take away one's control over one's life. You find you are talking about the issue not because you want to but because you can't help it. In other words, you have lost control.

Acknowledge it as an obsession and make the decision to begin taking back control of your own thoughts and behaviour. Whenever you find yourself on the verge of talking to your partner about the affair, don't! There will still be times when you *will* talk to him about it but begin rationing those times. Tell yourself you will only allow yourself to talk about it once a week for a while. Be firm with yourself. You already know that talking about it in the past hasn't resolved anything for you, hasn't taken away the pain and emptiness. So, tell yourself it's time to wean yourself off it. It would probably be helpful to have a series of weekly sessions with a counsellor. In that way, you could fulfil your need to talk about it while, at the same time, enlisting the counsellor's help to move beyond it. The crucial thing is that you find ways to stop being obsessive about it. By all means, do it at your own pace, but do it. You'll feel so much better when you're back in control of your own life.

28. When you lie awake at night going over and over conversations in your mind

This is part of the obsessiveness. You just can't stop thinking about it. When you lie awake at night going over and over things in your mind, you wish you could stop, but you can't. Let me say clearly and definitely: you can, and you must.

I think it would be helpful at this point if we took the time to focus on the emotional and psychological state of women once they discover their partner is having an affair. It is always important to be able to measure one's own reaction alongside what is said to be the "normal" reaction. As I said earlier, the immediate response most women have includes shock, disbelief, fear, grief, humiliation, anger and despair. Then, after a few weeks, the lingering, deeply distressing symptoms women describe are those of depression and anxiety.

Depression
The type of depression a woman experiences in these circumstances is sometimes called "reactive depression" or "dysthymia". It is not a major, deep-seated, long-term depression but one which has come on her as a reaction to her husband's betrayal. In other words, it is directly related to her recent circumstances and, if those circumstances could be resolved, her depression would lift.

What a woman feels at this time is a deep sense of loss, abandonment, emptiness, powerlessness and grief which can be expressed in any number of ways: withdrawal, crying, sobbing, loss of appetite or overeating, morbid thoughts, thoughts of suicide, disturbed sleep or insomnia, difficulty thinking and concentrating, feelings of worthlessness and guilt. All of these are symptomatic of depression and, while you will probably not experience all of the symptoms, you will experience some of them.

If you are depressed, it is important to realise you need to find a way to release all the feelings you have pressed down (de-pressed) inside you. What happened was your partner's betrayal rendered you helpless and you felt totally unable to make yourself feel better. You were experiencing a smorgasbord of emotions from which you could find no relief. After a short time, most of the friends and relatives you confided in began giving you subtle messages that they didn't want you talking about it "all the time". Or, even if there were people you could still talk to, it was never very satisfying for you because nobody could empathise with the depth of your agony and despair. So, you did the only thing open to you. You kept your emotions to yourself. You pushed them down deep inside you and hoped that time would heal. But now you're depressed. What you didn't realise was that the very act of de-pressing emotions causes depression. It follows, then, that the way to ease the depression is to get rid of the pent-up emotions by expressing them.

One way to release emotions is to do it by yourself—to cry, yell, scream, whatever you need to do—in private. But I must tell you that it is much more effective in terms of getting rid of depression if you do it with someone else. Find someone who will listen while you talk about how this terrible experience has affected you, someone who will be there while you cry and express all the emotions you've held inside. You'll need to have several talks, several sessions which could be quite emotionally draining for both of you. One talk and one cry is usually not enough. To avoid any guilt feelings about taking up too much of a friend's time, I strongly recommend that you find a counsellor or therapist (preferably a woman) and have as many sessions as you feel you need. Expressing how you feel in words and emotions will go a long way towards lifting your depression.

Anxiety

As described in Situation 25, there are two types of anxiety and both are related to the future. Normal anxiety is anxiety about something real which is about to happen, while abnormal anxiety doesn't seem to be related to anything. You ask yourself why you are feeling anxious or what it is that you are afraid of, and you have to admit that you don't know. These kinds of anxiety attacks or panic attacks, as they are sometimes called, are very puzzling but they are, nonetheless, real. Many women who discover their partner has been unfaithful experience anxiety and panic attacks for a time. While no one is certain about the cause of abnormal anxiety, we do know that it is often connected with a loss and/or feelings of powerlessness. Such experiences remind us with a jolt that nothing is certain in life, a realisation which throws us into deep anxiety.

You have experienced the loss of your relationship as you knew it and would do anything to get it back. You would do anything to make the nightmare of the last few weeks and months go away but you know you are powerless to change what has happened. In desperation, you try to find an explanation that will make you feel better. So you lie awake at night going over and over conversations and events. You do this for two reasons: to try to find a satisfactory explanation for what happened, and to try to work out what action to take.

Trying to find a satisfactory explanation

When our minds are obsessed with the question why, it is often because we find it too hard to accept the explanation that is staring us in the face. If a woman were to accept the true and simple explanation that her partner had an affair because he wanted to, she would find it too painful to bear. So she continues to ask why. She searches desperately for an explanation that will satisfy her. But there is none.

Asking why is usually fairly unproductive. It's like trying to have a conversation with a child who is in that inquisitive stage where, regardless of what you say or what explanation you give, the next question from the child's lips is always: Why?

When you say to yourself: "Yes, I realise he did it because he wanted to", your next question will inevitably be: "But why? Why did he want to?" You answer that question by thinking: "It was probably because he wasn't getting enough attention from me." Again, you will ask: "But why didn't he talk to me about needing more attention?" And so it will go on and on. It is much better to stop looking for an explanation, if you can. "Why?" will only lead you into more and more obsessive thinking. He did it, and that's that. There is no explanation that would make you feel better anyway.

Trying to work out what to do

You know you can't go on torturing yourself with thoughts of this and that. Why did he do it? What did they do together? Did he enjoy having sex with her? Was I so boring that he had to find someone else? Did I drive him away? Maybe if I had just . . . You know you have to stop that kind of thinking but there is another line of questioning you are equally obsessive about. It is this: What should I do? Should I leave him? Should I stay? How can I forgive him? How can I trust him? What would life be like without him? What would I do on my own? What about the children? How would all the relatives take it? If I stayed, what would life be like with him?

Each one of these questions brings with it hours of stressful to-ing and fro-ing in your mind and nothing ever gets resolved. Once you've gone through every question and imagined every possible scenario, what you find yourself doing is going right back and asking the same questions again and again.

When you lie awake at night focusing obsessively on Why did this happen? and What should I do?, what you are doing is trying to find relief from the pain and distress you feel. It is crucial that you look for relief in other ways. Of course, a certain amount of analysing and questioning has to happen but, once your thinking becomes obsessive, it is time to stop the thoughts and turn your attention to other ways of finding relief, as suggested below.

Suggestions for action

I want to acknowledge the fact that stopping the thoughts and turning one's attention to other things is in no way easy. Obsessive thoughts are extremely difficult to turn off. But, turn them off, you must.

Recognise your thoughts as obsessive

You will want to believe that the thinking you do after you get into bed is constructive thinking. It isn't! You will want to believe that going over and over things in your mind will one day result in a better understanding of your partner's betrayal. It won't! Once you can admit those truths to yourself and recognise that your need to understand has turned into an obsession, you will be on the path to releasing yourself from your self-imposed torture. It will help if you remind yourself that all the thinking in the world, all your attempts to explain it, will never result in an explanation which satisfies you. Admitting to yourself that it is a pointless exercise will make it easier for you to stop.

Get up out of bed

Whenever you find yourself lying awake going over and over things in your mind, get up out of bed. Don't lie there. You'll just get yourself more and more worked up, more and more anxious. Get up and do something. (The same is true when your obsessive thoughts occur during the day. Move. Do something else.) Read, maybe. Watch TV. Do a crossword or a jigsaw puzzle. If you are connected to the internet, get on the internet. Don't enter words like "marriage" or "betrayal" or "infidelity". The aim is to get your mind on a different track! Enter words like "travel" or "tennis" or "chimpanzees". Whatever you focus your search on, make sure it has no connection with the thing you're obsessing about and that it is something you are interested in. Then, when you go back to bed an hour or so later, you will go with other, more pleasant things, on your mind.

When you do go back into bed, the tendency will be for your mind to seize once again on your obsessive thoughts. That's the nature of an obsession. Every time that happens, it is up to you to exercise the strength of your mind to force the unpleasant thoughts out by deliberately replacing them with new thoughts. You may have to do that night after night and, sometimes, several times in the one night. Yes, you will be tired but you will not be as tired, and certainly not as distressed, as you would be if you continued to allow your obsessive thoughts to rule. Every time you get up and put your mind on other things, you are signalling to your mind that you will not be dominated by your obsessiveness.

Such determination will result, eventually, in your taking back control of your thoughts.

Learn the art of filling your mind with other thoughts

A very important lesson I learned several years ago was that my thoughts and behaviour did not always have to be spontaneous. For some strange reason, I used to think it was phony to *plan* to behave in a certain way (for example: "Next time my partner criticises me, I will say . . ."). I used to think it was wrong to direct my mind to push certain thoughts away and focus on others. But then I realised that I don't have to be at the mercy of my spontaneous thoughts and behaviours. I am the one who is in charge of my life and that means I ought to be able to decide what to think and how to behave.

I am not suggesting, of course, that we avoid all spontaneity because it's the ability to be, and to enjoy being, our spontaneous selves that makes us emotionally and psychologically healthy. What I am saying is that when our spontaneous thoughts and behaviour become a problem, it is then that we need to have the ability to make ourselves think and behave in new ways.

29. When you are overcome with anxiety/panic

An anxiety attack or panic attack can come upon a person at any time, day or night. Whenever it occurs, it is usually when one least expects it and it is always a most distressing experience. If you, as a result of discovering your partner's infidelity, are experiencing anxiety attacks, it is important that you recognise each attack for what it is. Instead of adding to your panic by saying: "Oh, my God. What's happening to me? What's wrong with me?", you must learn to say to yourself: "I know what's happening. It's all right. I'm having an anxiety attack. And I know it will pass." That way, you won't add more panic to the panic you are already feeling. The following discussion of symptoms will make your anxiety easier to recognise and, therefore, easier to deal with.

Symptoms of anxiety can be both emotional and physical. Among the most common emotional symptoms are: unexplained fear, panic, depression, dread, a feeling of impending doom and hypochondria. The most common physical symptoms are: pains in the chest, hyperventilation, churning stomach and dry mouth. Dr Claire Weekes in her book *Self Help for your Nerves** lists these and many more symptoms. You might want to look for that book in a bookshop or library. Other people writing about the condition include symptoms such as lightheadedness, a buzzing in the ears, blurred vision, trembling hands, twitching muscles, headaches.

Of course, in your struggle with anxiety, you will not experience every one of these symptoms but you will

---

* Claire Weekes (1962). *Self Help for your Nerves*. London: Angus & Robertson.

experience some of them. The important thing is that you recognise your own symptoms and, when they come upon you, identify them immediately as anxiety. It is important to add a word of caution. Some of the symptoms, such as pains in the chest, can be very worrying because of the fear that you could, indeed, be having a heart attack. The best course of action, in such cases, is to take that possibility seriously and consult your doctor immediately. If your doctor finds that your heart is sound and you have nothing to worry about physically, then you must identify the pains as symptoms of anxiety.

This is the first response you need to make on those occasions when you are overcome with anxiety: *recognise what is happening to you and name your symptoms as symptoms of anxiety.* This usually has the effect of reducing the anxiety and allowing you to take the appropriate steps to get on top of it. That brings us to the other response you need to make: *learn the steps required to get rid of your anxiety so that you can put those steps into practice whenever you need to.* The following suggestions for action are, in fact, steps in a treatment plan that works.

Suggestions for action

There are three main schools of thought about how to treat anxiety-sufferers. One is the medical model which posits anxiety as one of the symptoms of major depression and treats it with anti-depressant drugs. The second is the relaxation model which sees anxiety as closely related to stress and recommends relaxation, deep breathing and physical fitness as treatment strategies. The third and, I believe, the most effective is the Morita model, named after Japanese psychiatrist, Dr Shoma Morita, who developed his treatment plan in response to his own struggle with anxiety. My book, *Overcoming Anxiety*,* takes the Morita model and adapts it to Western culture.

The following are the six steps required by Morita therapy to ensure that you conquer your anxiety. Notice I didn't say: these are the six steps *suggested* by Morita therapy. I said *required*. Morita treatment is authoritarian in the sense that you cannot enter into the treatment plan half-heartedly. If you do, it won't work. Morita therapy is a cognitive-behavioural therapy. In order to change your behaviour (that is, your anxiety), you must believe in the strength of your mind to dominate your emotions. If you believe the treatment will work and throw yourself into it wholeheartedly, you will find relief from your anxiety.

Step one: Accept your anxiety

Although this first step seems really simple, people who suffer with anxiety tell me it is the hardest of all. How can you accept something that you hate? How can you welcome into your life something that you definitely don't want in your life? And they are right. The natural thing seems to be to fight against anything unpleasant. It seems sensible to push unpleasant feelings away. But Morita therapy says it is the very act of fighting against anxiety that keeps it alive. The more you focus on it, worry about it, hate it, try to work out how it started and how to get rid of it, the worse it will get. If you want its power over you to be broken, just accept it. For better or worse, accept it into your life. Say something like: "All right, then, I am an anxiety-sufferer. I'll accept that. I'm stuck with it till it decides to leave me, so I may as well

---

* Betty McLellan (1992). *Overcoming Anxiety: A positive approach to dealing with severe anxiety in your life*. Sydney: Allen & Unwin.

make the best of it." As soon as you genuinely accept anxiety, it begins to lose its power over you.

Step two: Learn about your anxiety

If the aim, as Morita therapy says, is for your mind to gain power over your anxiety, then you must learn as much as you can about it. Become as familiar with the condition as you can. Fill your mind with knowledge about it, because knowledge brings power and confidence. Knowledge about anxiety reduces its power to intimidate you. It reduces the fear.

Most doctors, counsellors and therapists seem only to know about the medical model or the relaxation model but, if you can find a professional person who is familiar with the Morita model, talk to them about it as a way of increasing your own understanding. Read as much as you can find about it. I particularly recommend my own book (mentioned above), which should be available in most libraries, or the book by Claire Weekes (also mentioned above). Both are helpful and practical resources.

Step three: Reinterpret your anxiety

Morita therapy encourages a positive reinterpretation of anxiety. Anxiety is only one side of the coin, they say. Instead of seeing yourself as someone who fears death, fears illness, fears old age, fears social and personal failure, look at the other side of the coin. If you fear death (for yourself or someone you love), it must mean that you have a desire for life. If you fear social and personal failure, it must be an indication that you desire to live your life in a meaningful and successful way. Reinterpreting your anxiety helps you change your attitude toward it which, in turn, helps you accept it.

Step four: Stop being preoccupied with your anxiety

To stop being preoccupied with your anxiety simply means: stop thinking about it. The first thing anyone does when they begin to experience abnormal anxiety or when they recognise some of the symptoms of anxiety beginning to appear, is focus their attention on it. "What's wrong with me? Why is this happening now?" Before they know it, their preoccupation with it has made it worse.

As I said earlier, as soon as you recognise a symptom, acknowledge it as anxiety. Instead of: "Why is this happening?", say to yourself: "It's all right. I know what this is. It's my anxiety." "Why" questions are problematic. Accept the fact that why it has come upon you doesn't matter. It *has* come upon you and your task is simply to acknowledge it and, then, to put it aside. Don't focus attention on it. Don't be preoccupied with it. Act as if it just isn't important enough to warrant your attention.

Did you notice those words "act as if"? I used those words intentionally because it will be an "act" at first. Ignoring your anxiety won't come naturally to you and it certainly won't be easy. You will have to force yourself to do it at first but once you experience the benefits of not allowing yourself to dwell on your anxiety, you will do it automatically.

Step five: Focus on actions (behaviour)
rather than feelings

Most of us women find it difficult to act without attention to our feelings. In Western societies, girls and women are encouraged to focus attention on our own and other people's emotions all the time. We are much better than men at expressing our own emotions and taking notice of how other people feel. Morita therapy insists that anxiety-sufferers learn how to turn off to their emotions and focus on actions and goals. They give an example of a person wanting to climb a ladder in order to do some work which needs to be done. The person is full of anxiety about climbing the ladder. According to Morita therapy, that person has two choices: either to stay on the ground and continue focusing on her anxiety or to climb the ladder giving full attention to the work waiting at the top. Focusing full attention on the task to be done, the person climbs the ladder and, somewhere toward the top of the ladder, realises her anxiety has disappeared.

Step six: Get on with your life

When you no longer feel compelled to focus obsessively on your anxiety and when you commit yourself to putting the above steps into practice every time any anxiety symptom appears, you will be free to get on with your life.

30. When you live every day with a gnawing feeling deep in the pit of your stomach

This is another symptom of anxiety and/or depression and, while there is very little more to say about it than that which I have already said, I want to focus on it briefly here. My reason for giving it special mention is that it is such a common feeling among people who have experienced loss.

If you experience this kind of sensation in your stomach, variously referred to as a gnawing feeling, a knot, a churning, an emptiness, you will know how very distressing it can be. It is, of course, a physical expression of the emotional trauma you are going through. The loss you experienced when you discovered your partner was having an affair, or when your partner announced he was leaving you, has provoked in you a deep sense of emptiness and powerlessness. When a woman describes to me the awful sensations she feels in her stomach, it always sounds like a description of emptiness or hollowness or hunger. Indeed, some women complain of putting on weight because they use food to try to fill their emptiness and satisfy their hunger. Others say that even though they feel really hungry, the thought of having to eat makes them feel sick. Eating too much or too little will not help.

Be aware that that emptiness in your stomach is a physical manifestation of how you are feeling and that, as soon as you begin to feel better, it will go away. The quickest way to begin to feel better is to give in to your feelings of grief and loss. Accept them. It's similar to the first step in dealing with anxiety (see Situation 29). Accept your loss. The more you fight against it and refuse to accept it, the worse you will feel. Many people find the prayer adopted by Alcoholics Anonymous very helpful in their struggle to accept a loss. The first line of the prayer goes like this: "God grant me the serenity to accept the things I cannot change . . .". When something happens in your life over which you have no control, the only avenue open to you is to accept it. Give in to it humbly and with serenity. This marks the first step on the road to feeling better.

Judy Horacek (1992/2003). *Life on the Edge.*
Melbourne: Spinifex, p. 33.

It will take a while for you to get back to feeling like your old self, physically and emotionally, but be patient. Take your time. Don't try to rush it. The following list of suggestions, which do not need further elaboration, will result in the gradual easing of your feelings of emptiness and powerlessness and the restoring of a sense of peace and well-being.

Suggestions for action

Accept your loss

Grieve for your loss

Keep yourself inwardly as calm as you can

Eat healthy foods

Focus on keeping physically fit

Renew old friendships with women

*Calmly look for opportunities to develop
new friendships*

*Enjoy your new-found sense of well-being
when it comes*

Judy Horacek (1992/2003). *Life on the Edge.*
Melbourne: Spinifex, p. 83.

31. Knowing you can neither live with him nor live without him

Should I? Shouldn't I? Will I? Won't I? Indecision is a very distressing thing. Women tell me that following the discovery of their partner's infidelity they spent a lot of time and emotional energy trying to figure out what to do. They felt so hurt, so incensed by his betrayal, that they could not bear the thought of staying with him. So they decided! It was over! And they felt good about their decision.

But, then, within a matter of hours, they had changed their minds. They thought about how many years they had invested in the relationship, how comfortable and enjoyable it could be at times and how much love they still felt for their partner. No. They couldn't leave him. So they decided to stay and felt fairly certain they could live with that decision and find happiness again. Then, within hours, they were back to leaving again. Back and forth. Back and forth.

Indecision can make you feel like you're going crazy. If only it was clear cut. If only your partner was a complete bastard all the time, the decision would be much easier. But most men are bastards only some of the time! The rest of the time they're okay and, some of the time, they are even great to be with.

In order to help you in your decision-making, I want to spend some time here looking into some of the major considerations, and doing that in a fairly rational way. Now, there is a long-running debate in our society about whether it is better to be emotional or rational. Some people maintain that all decisions must be made rationally, that emotions shouldn't come into decision-making. I disagree. I believe every decision must take account of both emotion and fact. Of course, it is easier to make decisions if you ignore your emotions and focus only on the facts, but how can you ignore emotions when your emotions are very much involved? That's why it is easy for someone on the outside (a friend or relative) to say: "Of course, you should leave him. There's no question about it." It's easy for someone on the outside to make a cool, rational judgement about what you should do because they have no emotional investment in your partner or in the relationship. You, on the other hand, have a huge emotional investment.

Acknowledging that both thought and emotion will influence your ultimate decision I, nevertheless, ask you to begin by exploring the following questions rationally.

When does the decision about whether to leave or stay with one's partner usually arise?
There are three main scenarios for a woman:
1.   She has fallen in love with someone else.
2.   She discovers her partner has been having an affair. If he leaves her for the other woman, there is no decision for her to make but, if he chooses to finish the affair and stay with his partner, she then has to decide if she wants to continue the relationship.
3.   She is worn down by her partner's immature attitudes and behaviour day by day. There are any number of day-to-day situations which cause women to consider whether or not to leave—his refusal to communicate; his lying; his ridiculing; his violence toward her; his emotional, physical or sexual abuse of the children; his excessive drinking or drug-taking; his excessive gambling; his spending of their joint money without consultation; his illegal activities; and so on.

What effect does a woman's indecision have on her?
Of the three scenarios mentioned above, I want to focus only on the second and third because the power dynamics in the first scenario are quite different from those in the other two. In the first, the woman is operating from a position of power, that is, it is her own behaviour which has brought her to the point of having to make a decision. My interest, in the context of this book, is to focus on decision-making from a position of powerlessness, that is, when a woman is thrown into the need to make a decision because of her partner's behaviour.

When a woman puts pressure on herself to make a decision about continuing or ending her relationship, the effect on her differs with differing circumstances. If she has discovered her partner has been having an affair, there is a suddenness about the discovery which tends to throw her into turmoil. She agonises over what to do but there is an urgency about it. The depression and anxiety which have come upon her make her desperate to do something quickly to restore her sense of worth and stability. Should she leave? Should she stay? She. thinks about it obsessively day and night. But she can't decide.

If, on the other hand, it is a situation where she has simply had enough of her partner's destructive attitudes and behaviour, she is more likely to spend time making plans. Her disenchantment with the relationship has grown steadily over a long period of time so there isn't the same sense of urgency as there is with the sudden discovery of infidelity. Many women who become aware over time of their growing unhappiness tend to make plans and bide their time. They know their choices are either to leave him or to find a way to ignore his childishness and pursue their own lives while remaining in the relationship. This latter option entails sidelining one's partner emotionally, making a decision to divest his objectionable behaviour of any power to evoke emotion. It means, of course, that the relationship is virtually over even though her decision is to continue living in the same house.

When a woman is caught up in indecision, it usually has the effect of immobilising her. She feels as if her life is stuck and, although she sees herself continuing to do the daily chores, she is aware that she is not really "living". It is for that reason that fantasies about what you will do "one day" can be helpful. At least, when you are making plans in your head, you save yourself from feeling totally powerless and immobilised. The negative side of having such fantasies and making such plans is that it can simply be an aid to indecision, a way of delaying decision-making indefinitely or escaping from it altogether. While you keep making plans, there doesn't seem to be a need to decide or act. The hard part is changing fantasy into reality.

How do men respond to confrontation about their behaviour?

A woman's decision about what to do is usually affected by her partner's attitude once he has been confronted. Some men make it clear that they just don't care, while others want you to see how sorry they are. If your partner's attitude is that he doesn't care, if he laughs off what you say, if he gets angry and tells you that what he does is none of your business, if he tells you you can leave if you don't like the way he is, your decision is made easier. You really must leave. This doesn't mean you *will* leave, though, because you may have other reasons for staying and putting up with his arrogant and destructive behaviour toward you. But, at least, your decision about what you *ought* to do is clear. While staying in a destructive situation is not the best outcome, it is better for you, psychologically, to say: "I know I ought to leave, but I won't", than to be stuck in indecision: "Will I? Won't I?"

A response which is easier to bear, though not always easier to deal with, is the response which begins with: "I'm sorry." Those men who express remorse in response to a woman's confrontation, either about their infidelity or their unacceptable behaviour, come in three varieties. First, there are those who say they are sorry and whose subsequent behaviour seems to demonstrate real remorse. They seem genuinely to care about the pain and distress they have caused their partner. They acknowledge the need to change their self-centred, self-absorbed, self-seeking attitudes and behaviour to become more other-focused, more concerned about the well-being of their partner and children. In order to give themselves the greatest chance of effecting such a change, they may seek the help of a counsellor or therapist and persevere till they see results.

A woman who sees her partner genuinely struggling to change, putting time and effort into developing a new maturity, is likely to find the decision to stay in the relationship reasonably easy to make.

Second, there are those men who say they are sorry and who make all kinds of promises, but whose remorse seems to end after about a week. At the time of the confrontation, they did seem to care about how their partner was feeling but expected that everything would return to normal once they had said they were sorry. When it doesn't, they become impatient and, sometimes, angry. In these situations, a woman's decision is much more difficult to make. Knowing that his behaviour will probably revert to the way it was, she asks herself if she really wants to continue in a relationship which plays out the same cycle over and over: arrogant behaviour and/or infidelity—confrontation—remorse—best behaviour; then back to: arrogant behaviour and/or infidelity—confrontation—remorse—best behaviour . . . and so on.

Finally, there are those men who say they are sorry and do everything they can to demonstrate real remorse but who say they "can't" promise that their behaviour will change because it is out of their control. These men want to believe, and they want you to believe, that they only behave the way they do because they can't help it. It is a "problem" they have, and all they can promise is that they will work on it. Very convenient, indeed! Meanwhile, they can slip up as often as they like because they have convinced themselves that they are not responsible. Some mysterious force is making them do it! What they are actually doing is setting up a situation where you are not able to be too angry with them because they have a "problem". If you do express the anger you feel, you are seen to be heartless and uncaring. They have a "problem" and you are supposed to feel sorry for them. You are supposed to express sympathy, commit yourself to "helping" them with their "problem" and, above all, you are to be patient. To lend legitimacy to their theory, they will talk to you about their childhood, about how nobody loved them or everybody treated them badly. All they want from you, they will say, is understanding and patience. What happens then? Well, they continue to "work on" their problem for years. As a matter of fact, there never comes a time when they are "cured", never a time when they can promise you they will change their behaviour. Not surprisingly, there will be times during those years when they have another affair or another outburst of violence or whatever it was that you confronted them about. But you are not supposed to express anger about that. You are not supposed to leave them. You are supposed to understand that they have a problem which they are doing their best to overcome.

This whole attempt at an explanation for their betrayal is simply a refusal on their part to put effort into cleaning up their act. They want the right to continue pursuing what both worlds offer—the security of a committed relationship and the freedom to do exactly as they please.

When a man tells you he really wants to change but his "problems" take over and *make* him do what he doesn't want to do, don't believe him. It's nonsense—and you must tell him so. Many men who use this excuse actually believe it, so it is crucial that you let your partner know that you are not buying his explanation. It is nothing more than an excuse to continue doing what he wants to do. People with any intellectual ability at all can change their behaviour if they want to badly enough. Let him know that your expectation is that he will put effort into changing.

Suggestions for action

When you are plagued with indecision, the immediate and urgent requirement is that you *make a decision*. How will you do that?

Weigh up the pros and cons

It is often a good idea to stop and actually write down all your reasons for staying with your partner and all your reasons for leaving. Getting things down on paper can relieve the confusion that comes from trying to hold everything in your head. Once you've written your reasons down, preferably in two columns side by side, you can look at them objectively and make a comparison.

I don't mean to imply that, once you have done that, the decision will be easy. You still have your emotions to deal with. You still have your fears about being alone, your anxieties about starting again, your desire to stay and make it work, your longing to be a happy family, your concerns about the children. Many women say they know what they should do but can't bring themselves to do it. In other words, their emotions complicate the issue and make decision-making very difficult.

Anticipate the future

Weighing up the pros and cons in relation to your options of leaving or not leaving includes a process of anticipating the outcomes of each option. "If I leave, what will my life be like?" Think through exactly what you would do. Anticipate all the steps you would take: how you would tell your partner; what his response would be; how you would feel; how you would tell the children; how you would cope with their opinions and feelings; who you would get to help you move; where you would move to; how you would manage financially; how you would cope with other people's criticism. Anticipate every detail. This is essential because it is actually a practice-run. If you can't manage it in the practice-run, then don't do it. Don't leave until you are satisfied you can do it successfully. Go through it again in your head. Talk to a counsellor at a Women's Centre, if there is one available. Get legal advice. Talk to a friend you know you can trust. Practise in your head until you are confident you could manage.

Then, look at the other option and anticipate the outcomes of choosing that option. "If I stay, what will my life be like?" Think through exactly what you would do if you decided to stay: how you would feel about yourself; how you would go about insisting that your partner see a counsellor with a view to changing some of his attitudes and behaviour; what you would do if he refused; how you would develop a healthier, happier atmosphere for yourself and the children; how you would endure the relationship if nothing changed; what changes you would make in your own life regardless of your partner's attitudes; how you would cope with other people's criticism. Anticipate every detail because, again, this is a practice-run. Talk to a counsellor or a friend you know you can trust. The decision to stay is, in some ways, more difficult than the decision to leave. Either way, you will need all the support you can get.

If you still can't decide—don't leave

When your indecision (Will I? Won't I?) develops into an obsession—something you can't stop thinking about—you must stop the indecision. If you find you can't decide, it is crucial that you decide to stay where you are.

Of course, there will be people who will criticise you for "letting him get away with what he did" to you, but there would be just as many people who would criticise you if you decided to leave. I always say: when you can't please everybody, you may as well please yourself. *You* are the one in the middle of all this and *you* must be the one to decide what you will do, but don't act hastily. If you're having difficulty deciding, then decide to stay where you are for the time being.

And one other thing. Don't criticise yourself for deciding to stay. Don't see it as inaction on your part. See it as a decision you have made after weighing up the pros and cons, because that is exactly what it is. You are not just a passive recipient of whatever happens to you but an assertive decision-maker acting on a decision you have made. If, at a later date, the need for a different decision arises, then you will look at it again at that time.

Living with Mr Nice Guy

32. When friends and family tell you how lucky you are

Sometimes, all you want is a bit of support from family and friends but, so often, when you pour your heart out to someone, they end up telling you how lucky you are! They have no idea how frustrating it is living twenty-four hours a day with a man who is immature, self-centred and self-absorbed, or whose way of dealing with issues is to withdraw into himself. Or, they have no idea how terrifying it can be living with a man who is vindictive, explosive and violent. Regardless of how your partner expresses his immaturity, being in a relationship with a man who acts in any one of those ways—self-centred or withdrawn or violent—can be soul-destroying for any woman. At first you think you can handle it, but being in that situation year after year with no indication that he will ever change, that he will ever see the need to grow up and become a responsible adult, can cause a woman to feel desperate.

There are times when you long to talk to someone just to get a bit of support. You're not asking for advice. You're not asking for anyone to pass judgement on your partner or on you. You just need to talk, to cry on someone's shoulder, as it were, and feel that someone has acknowledged your pain and distress.

Women who live with men who are seen as "nice guys" are commonly told how lucky they are. If you live with a man who is capable of gentleness, sensitivity and concern, or if your partner is a man who values communication, other women will envy you. You will be seen as "lucky". Some men who have a reputation for being sensitive and caring really are sensitive and caring. And they work hard with their partners to develop a relationship which is fair to both of them. Others, however, put on a show and *hope to be noticed* for their sensitivity. These are the men who let it be known that they are prepared to "babysit" (their own children) while their partner goes out. When he does this, she is said to be "lucky". These are the men who expect a pat on the back for "helping" with the housework.

It's ironic, isn't it? When a woman stays home with the children six nights out of seven every week, her partner is never told that he is lucky to have such a good wife. But if he stays home with the children one night in seven, she is said to be lucky and it is implied that she ought to be grateful.

The language used in these instances is very revealing. When a man "babysits" his own children, "helps out" with the housework, does the dishes "for you", it is clear that all of these tasks are actually seen as the sole responsibility of a woman and that you are, indeed, lucky if the man in your life condescends to help.

This attitude is extremely frustrating for women, and sometimes you just need to express your thoughts and feelings about the injustice of it all—and you need someone to listen and care. Most people, sadly, don't want to know about it. They don't want to hear anything negative. In fact, they won't listen. Many people, it seems, have a low tolerance for emotional pain and, when you talk to them about the desperation you feel, they have to turn it into something positive. I call it the "don't worry —be happy" syndrome. Instead of empathising with you, instead of being with you and letting you talk and cry it out of your system, they turn it into something positive. "But he's so good with the kids, isn't he? You're really lucky he's such a good father."

What a sad indictment on our society that a woman who lives with a man who mistreats her is supposed to feel lucky because he doesn't mistreat the children. You hear it all the time. As unjust as it is, a woman in a relationship with a man who doesn't beat her up is supposed to feel "lucky"; women who weren't sexually assaulted in childhood feel "lucky"; women in relationships with men who live and breathe their work and give no time at all to their family feel "lucky" because their partner is a good provider.

Such a situation speaks volumes about men and masculinity, doesn't it? If women are supposed to feel lucky when they aren't beaten up, ignored or mistreated by their partner, if women and children are supposed to feel lucky to get through life without being raped or sexually assaulted, it says that male violence and male arrogance have become the norm. It says that we are to *expect* violence and arrogance from men and that, if those things don't happen, we are "lucky".

I don't mind admitting that I worry a lot about the increasing level of immaturity, self-centredness and violence we are seeing in men and boys. Lots of women worry about it. There are men, too, for whom it is a great concern. But there doesn't seem to be agreement on what to do to turn the situation around. Many people throw the whole responsibility back on women and, in particular, on mothers. They say the answer lies in bringing boys up differently and the responsibility for that lies, of course, with mothers. Mothers must learn how to encourage boys to be more thoughtful of others, they say. Mothers must discourage violence and teach their boys non-violent ways of dealing with things. I know those who suggest this solution mean well but, when boys are surrounded with examples of male arrogance and male violence every day, any teaching to the contrary from mothers pales into insignificance. When a boy has a choice between his father's example of arrogance, domination, self-centredness, and freedom to do as he pleases and his mother's input about humility, cooperation, caring, and acting responsibly, it isn't too hard to figure out which option a boy would find more attractive.

Instead of throwing all the responsibility on mothers to rescue boys from the declining standards of masculinity, there are others who say it is up to *men* to begin setting a better example. Of course it is! And those of us who share a concern about the ethical decline in masculinity need to let our voices be heard. All of us, women and men, who object to living in a society where women and children are supposed to feel "lucky" if they are not mistreated by a man, must say so at every opportunity. We object! If enough women and men object to the downward trend, if enough women and men insist that immature men give less attention to satisfying their own selfish wants and more attention to setting a good example for the next generation of boys, then we will reverse the downward trend. It's called "People Power".

Suggestions for action

Don't accept the label "lucky"

No one who is mistreated or ignored or put down is lucky. It is important that you believe that. Those family members and friends who insist on putting a positive spin on your frustration and distress are actually more interested in their own comfort than yours. They feel uncomfortable when you talk about your sadness and frustration so they imply that you don't really mean what you're saying, you don't really feel the way you say you feel. When you get a "don't worry—be happy" response, the only interpretation you can put on it is that the person you are confiding in is more interested in their own feelings than yours.

Look for someone to talk to who knows how to empathise

Empathy is the ability to get outside one's own feelings and problems, and feel with someone else. Lots of people seem to be so self-focused that they allow their own needs to intrude on every interaction they ever have. In order to be a good help and support to others, we need to learn the art of putting our own problems and fears aside and being fully there for others when they need us.

When you are at your wit's end and just need someone to talk to, look for someone who is mature enough to let you talk and cry without giving you advice, without imposing their opinion or judgement on you. Look for someone who doesn't feel compelled to tell you how lucky you are.

Object loudly to the decline in masculine standards

If we want men to set a better example for our sons and grandsons, we are going to have to *insist* on it. Women must stop taking the blame. Women must stop trying to figure out where *we* are going wrong in bringing up our boys and accept that it is the poor example of so many men that is to blame. We must object loudly, and at every opportunity, until men take responsibility for the kind of example they set.

33. When you are told that his behaviour is your responsibility

Sometimes, when a woman turns to friends or family for support, the response she gets is even worse than being told how lucky she is. Sometimes she is actually criticised for the fact that her partner is mistreating her, because his behaviour is said to be her responsibility. If he drinks too much, it must be her fault. If he gambles too much, if he is obsessed with his work, if he has an affair, if he withdraws and keeps to himself, if he is violent or threatens violence, it must be her fault.

When you are the victim, the one who has to put up with his mistreatment, you don't expect to be blamed. You expect some support from those closest to you. But "blaming the victim" is actually quite common. Often it is the result of twisted logic. For example, you may confide in your parents who you know love you and want you to be happy. Instead of simply empathising with you, which is all you're asking from them, they feel they have to *do* something. What can they do? They know that your partner is so self-absorbed that he will never change. As a consequence, they know that blaming him or speaking to him about changing his behaviour would be pointless. So they blame you! That's something they *can* do. Regardless of how devastating that is for you, at least they feel they have done something.

What a tragedy! Blaming the victim is always such a tragedy because it only serves to heap more pain on someone who is already experiencing too much pain. Injustice is added to injustice.

Suggestions for action

Don't accept responsibility

No one can be held responsible for another person's behaviour. Men often try to excuse themselves for arrogant or violent behaviour by saying their partner provoked them. "If she hadn't said that, I wouldn't have hit her." Or "She drove me away. If she had agreed to have sex more often, I wouldn't have found someone else." No one is responsible for their partner's behaviour. In the first example, the woman is only responsible for what she said to him. *He* is responsible for his violent reaction. In the second example, the woman is only responsible for being honest about her sexual needs and saying "no" when she didn't want to have sex. *He* is responsible for choosing to have an affair. Don't ever accept the blame because, if you are prepared to accept it, even only once or twice, it creates a situation where it is easier to blame you every time. (For a more detailed discussion of blame and guilt, see Situation 36.)

Look for someone to talk to who will give you support, not blame

When you are feeling bad because of the way your partner treats you or because of his attitude toward you, you do not need the added trauma of being made to feel you are responsible for your own pain. As suggested in Situation 32, look for someone to talk to who knows how to empathise. What you need is support, not blame.

34. Living with a man who puts on a good show for others

What do you do with a man who is extremely difficult to live with but who puts on a great show for others? Mr Nice Guy. Mr Considerate Husband. Mr Caring Father. As far as anyone outside the home is concerned, you are so lucky to be living with such an all-round good bloke. And when you need to talk to a friend or relative about how difficult things are and how unhappy you are, forget it! The problem must be *you* because all they see is a very nice guy. How frustrating!

This is not an uncommon situation, of course. Lots of women experience the frustration of living with a man who seems particularly practised in the art of putting on a respectable front. As a matter of fact, we all know of men in public life, men who are publicly admired for what they do and what they presume to stand for, who then are revealed to be perpetrators of violence in the home, charged with rape or sexual harassment or sexual abuse of children, involved in drunken brawls or lewd behaviour, taking drugs, or taking bribes. Such men include politicians, presidents, prime ministers, churchmen, sportsmen, lawyers, actors, doctors, therapists, welfare workers, all of whom go to a lot of trouble to put on a show of being good upstanding, dependable leaders in the community. When their real characters and motives are finally exposed, we can't help feeling let down. And we worry about our sons and grandsons who, so often, take sportsmen and other male leaders as their role models.

I know of a man who puts on a show of being a caring, concerned pillar of the community. Apart from his job in a law firm, he is a member of an active service club and gives much of his spare time to volunteer work with charities. On the surface, one would say he is a mature, selfless, caring man. But, over the years, I have had his first wife, then his second wife, then his third wife talk to me about his violence in the home, the reign of terror he has subjected his partners and children to over many years. I took it upon myself, a few years ago, to confront this man about his violence and he admitted it. But, in his opinion, it was never his fault. His partner or child always provoked him. There was always a reason, an excuse for his violence which meant he never had to feel guilty and he never had to think about changing. He excused himself. Consequently, he is probably still being violent at home while continuing to receive accolades in the community for his public show of selflessness and concern for others.

Then, there are men who are always the life of any party. They are known for their sense of humour, their ability to socialise and their ability to help others relax and enjoy themselves. Women who are fighting off boredom with their decent, but dull, husbands find themselves secretly envying the wives of these men who seem so alive and vibrant. It follows that, if those women were approached by one of the wives who needed to talk about how "the life of the party" treats her and the children at home, they would find it difficult to believe and would be slow to offer support.

When you are the only adult who knows what your partner is really like, it can be extremely frustrating. You find yourself longing for his true self to be revealed, but that may never happen. Some women make the mistake of taking every opportunity to criticise their partner to others in the hope that others will see what he is really like. The problem is that, unless they see it for themselves, they will have difficulty believing you. As a matter of fact, it is more likely that they will see you as the one with the problem. You will be identified as bitter and twisted, as having a chip on your shoulder. And, ironically, they will feel sympathy for your partner for having to put up with you.

While you haven't been able to get him to change the way he behaves at home you could, perhaps, minimise your frustration and anger by reducing the number of times you go to social gatherings with him. If you don't have to witness his phony social behaviour, you won't have that constant reminder of the difference between the way he presents to others and the way he is at home. One of the reasons why his social behaviour is so annoying is that it demonstrates to you that he does have the ability to be kind, to be a fun person, to stop focusing on himself and be interested in others. He *can* do it. He just chooses not to do it at home.

Suggestions for action

Don't let his deception wear you down

It is true that having to witness your partner's deceptive behaviour whenever you are out with him socially, will wear you down. You will feel angry and deeply distressed at the injustice of it all. Here he is acting as if butter wouldn't melt in his mouth, receiving all the attention and adulation anyone could want, being hailed as a really nice guy. You, on the other hand, are full of cynicism and anger because you are the only one who knows what he's really like.

It is very important that you find a way to release yourself from the distress and anger such situations cause you. One way, which I have already mentioned, is to stop going out with him publicly. Stop attending social gatherings. If he wants to go, he can go by himself. Another way of reducing the effect his phony social behaviour has on you is to continue socialising with him, but to make up your mind that his behaviour isn't going to bother you. Have a good laugh inside yourself when you see him "performing". If he wants to live as a split person, if he wants to live with that level of dishonesty, you must develop the attitude that it is his choice and it doesn't matter to you. *You* know he's living a lie and, at some level, *he* must know he's living a lie, so be satisfied with that. Just stand back and observe him putting on his show. Expect it and you won't be surprised. Laugh about it inside yourself. Keep yourself physically separated from him as much as possible in those situations and be determined to enjoy socialising with your friends. If you can develop such an attitude, you'll find that his behaviour will no longer have the power to eat away at you.

A third option is to leave him. If you try the first two options and they don't work for you and, if you can find no way to tolerate his dishonest behaviour without it causing you depression and seething anger, you must consider leaving him.

Don't waste time trying to expose him

As I already mentioned, some women who find themselves in this situation are so determined to expose their partner's double life to friends and acquaintances that they take it on as a kind of crusade. They become obsessed with trying to get others to see what he's really like. Don't do it. It's a waste of time. Such a crusade is beneath you. And all it will do is diminish you in the eyes of your friends.

Don't let his deception change your personality

When you long to expose him and allow yourself to become obsessed by thoughts of how you might do that, it can change your personality. Instead of the happy, free, caring person you used to be, you can easily become nasty, vindictive and disturbed. Don't let that happen. That can lead to serious depression. It can also lead to a situation where your friends no longer want to associate with you and you are isolated. Your battle to expose him can become a very lonely battle. It's not worth it. It is much better for you if you can find a way to ignore his deception.

Find someone to talk to who believes you and will support you

As pointed out in Situations 32 and 33, it is always important to find one person—a friend or a counsellor—who believes you and will support you during those times when you need a shoulder to cry on. No matter how good a show your partner puts on for others, you know what he's like at home and, with the support of someone who believes you, you can come to a decision about how to handle your distress.

Jacky Fleming (1992). *Never Give Up*. London: Penguin.

Woman-Self:
becoming strong,
growing stronger

35. When your problems seem to go on and on

Take a day off from your worries occasionally. Go shopping. Go to the movies. Go swimming. Have fun. Give yourself permission to stop thinking about your problems for one whole day. You'll find it so refreshing.

Remember, your problems will still be there tomorrow. So, just for today, relax and have fun!

Judy Horacek (1998). *Woman with Altitude*.
Rydalmere, NSW: Hodder, p. 14.

36. When you feel burdened with guilt

It's strange, but true, that women living with immature men often feel burdened with guilt. A woman who is unhappy and frustrated in her relationship can find herself feeling guilty about many things.

In the first place, she can feel guilty about not having a good relationship. She blames herself. She looks around at her friends and acquaintances and convinces herself that they are all happy (even though she has no idea what actually goes on between them in the privacy of their homes). She tells herself she is the only one who hasn't been able to make her relationship work, and she feels guilty. The attitude in the community doesn't help, either. Even though one often hears people saying things like "It takes two to tango", there is still a strongly held belief out there that it is the *woman's* responsibility to make a relationship work.

Second, a woman can feel guilty because she hasn't succeeded in "training" her partner. Most self-help books about relationships are aimed at women (because the authors know men aren't interested in reading such things). The fact that they are aimed at women automatically gives women the message that it is their responsibility to work toward developing a better relationship. The image these books portray is that a man is as he is. He probably won't change. He can be difficult to live with. He can be immature. He can be violent. But it doesn't matter. It is the woman's responsibility to put effort into understanding how he is and work around him. Such books make out that men are eminently trainable and that, if you have not been able to train "your man", you haven't been trying hard enough. They make it sound so easy that those women who have not been successful in getting their partner to make some changes in his attitudes and behaviour feel guilty. What the authors of these books fail to acknowledge is that immature, self-centred men are determined to be exactly how they want to be and any suggestion of change is met with strong and prolonged resistance.

Third, a woman can feel guilty for not being happy, for not being satisfied with what she has in life. She looks at her immature partner and her unsatisfactory relationship and reminds herself that this is her lot in life. She tells herself she *should* be satisfied. There's no point wanting more, when more is what you're not going to get! Even though it is appropriate to feel dissatisfied when you are in a situation which is unsatisfying, many women feel guilty when they long for more.

Finally, a woman can feel guilty because she believes she must be provoking her partner into treating her badly. The more she tries to figure out why he is so rude and uncaring, the more confused she becomes. To accept the most obvious explanation of all, which is simply that he is an immature man who has no concern for anyone but himself, would be too painful for her. If she believed that, she would have to admit that he will never change and that her situation will never improve for as long as she is with him, so she chooses to blame herself. She prefers to believe there must be something she is doing to make him behave the way he does.

Why is it that women find it so easy to accept blame and feel guilty? From a psychological viewpoint, it is crucial that we seek to understand the concept of guilt and make a determined effort to stop feeling guilty when we have not, in fact, done anything wrong. It is emotionally, psychologically and spiritually unhealthy to do so. In an attempt to shed a bit of light on the concept of guilt, I want to do three things: first, attempt to define it;

second, look at women's relationship to guilt; and finally, consider the need to differentiate between feeling guilty and being guilty.

Defining guilt

First question: What is guilt? A simple dictionary definition states that guilt comes from having committed an offence. In other words, a guilty person is one who has done something wrong, one who is at fault, one who is to blame. Other people, writing about guilt, remind us that it is never as simple as that. They confirm what you and I already know from our own experience, which is that any definition of guilt must take into account the difference between *feeling* guilty and actually *being* guilty. The paradox is that, often, the one who is guilty doesn't feel guilty and the one who feels guilty is not, in fact, guilty. A more accurate definition, therefore, would be: guilt is a sense of wrongdoing, involving thoughts or actions, arising out of real or imagined violation of moral or social standards.

Guilt is a feeling, an emotional attitude. Sometimes it is grounded in reality and sometimes it springs from one's imagination. When you really have done something wrong, guilt feelings are appropriate; but when you have done nothing wrong guilt feelings are inappropriate and, indeed, unhealthy.

Women and guilt

Second question: Why is it that women are always finding something to feel guilty about? It's true, isn't it? In my book, *Beyond Psychoppression,** I pointed out that there are three attitudes toward guilt which are

---

* Betty McLellan (1995). *Beyond Psychoppression: A Feminist Alternative Therapy*. Melbourne: Spinifex, p. 65.

harmful to emotional health. One is when we are guilty but refuse to admit it. Another is when we are guilty and wallow in it instead of confessing and moving beyond it. And a third is when we are not guilty but choose to feel guilty anyhow.

What I notice as I observe people in a variety of situations is that the first attitude is common among men and the third is common among women. And there seems to be a connection between the two. Whenever a man refuses to take responsibility for his bad behaviour, there always seems to be a woman who steps in and feels guilty on his behalf. Why do we do that? I think it's because women have been socialised to be martyrs and carers and rescuers of men. We are expected to feel guilty, and we do it almost without thinking. For the sake of our own mental health and happiness, however, it is imperative that we stop feeling guilty when we are not guilty. Such behaviour has three consequences: it keeps us feeling bad about ourselves and robs us of the strength to confront those who are really guilty; it necessitates our living a lie; and it supports injustice by allowing the actual guilty person to pretend he is not guilty.

Healthy attitude toward guilt
Third question: How can we develop a healthier attitude toward guilt? A healthy relationship to guilt involves the following:
- When you *are* guilty, you should feel guilty.
- When you *are* guilty, you should admit your wrong-doing to yourself and others.
- When you *are* guilty, you should apologise and do all you can to make things right. If you are genuinely sorry and have demonstrated that by your actions, you must then attempt to leave it behind you. Wallowing in it, going over and over it in your mind

or in conversation with others, is pointless. Forgive yourself, stop focusing on it, and just get on with your life.

• When you *are not* guilty, you must not feel guilty. When guilt feelings creep in automatically, you must tell yourself there is absolutely no reason to feel guilty. Refuse to be dragged down by the need to take on someone else's guilt. Remind yourself that you are doing everything in your power to live a good life, to be a mature person, and to have mature relationships and that, consequently, there is no reason to waste time and energy feeling guilty.

Suggestions for action

Develop the ability to distinguish between real guilt and imagined guilt

Be prepared to acknowledge that there is a difference and that feeling guilty doesn't always mean that you *are* guilty. Spend time thinking about all the times you felt guilty on behalf of your partner and remind yourself of the fact that taking on his guilt has never resulted in improved behaviour on his part.

Don't waste your energy feeling guilty when you're not guilty

Make a promise to yourself that you will only feel guilty when you *are* guilty. That way, you will have a much greater chance of being emotionally and psychologically healthy.

When you are guilty, be mature enough to admit it

When you have done or said something with the intention of hurting someone else, admit it, apologise, and ask for forgiveness.

Get the blame right

Blame is a very important issue for mental health and happiness. If blame is not directed appropriately, then justice is not done and emotional health is impeded. Women in relationships with immature men often get the blame wrong and wonder why their partner's behaviour never changes. When a man continually behaves in an arrogant and self-centred way, women often search for someone to blame. A convenient person to blame, of course, is his mother. If she had cared about him, if she had brought him up to respect women, if she hadn't spoiled him, if she hadn't been so hard on him, he wouldn't be like this. Other people and events are also blamed: his father, his sister, his first wife, stress, unemployment, serving in the war, and so it goes on. If you find yourself blaming these or other people and circumstances for your partner's immature behaviour, then you have got the blame wrong.

Another common way women get the blame wrong is to blame themselves, as discussed above. I say as firmly as I can that the only person to blame for your partner's bad behaviour is your partner himself. To look for someone else to blame is to excuse him and, if you excuse him, you are robbing yourself of any hope that he will ever change. Get the blame right. Blame the one who is blameworthy. If he accepts responsibility for his actions, he will have taken the first step toward change.

Enjoy freedom from guilt

If you confess when you are guilty and seek the other person's forgiveness, and if you refuse to feel guilty when you are not guilty, then you will be free from guilt. Enjoy the feeling. A mature person who has good intentions toward others will very rarely experience the need to feel guilty. You may wonder what you'll do with all that time and energy previously spent on worrying and feeling bad! You may also wonder what there will be to think about when you don't have bad thoughts about yourself to dwell on! Try it. You'll find life is so much more enjoyable and positive.

37. When you struggle to forgive

If you are like most women I know, you'd really like to be able to forgive your partner, no matter what he does. But sometimes it's difficult. I want to ask: Why do we struggle so hard to forgive? Over the last thirty years, our society has seen a growing emphasis on the need to forgive. The church preaches forgiveness. Therapists encourage forgiveness. Popular psychology and self-help books urge forgiveness. And those who do not or cannot forgive someone who has wronged them are made to feel they are committing a sin, are emotionally sick or, at the very least, are bitter and uncompromising. Forgiveness is made out to be more important even than justice. It doesn't seem to matter if justice is done in any given situation, so long as you forgive. That's the message we are getting from society, and I find it worrying.

The issue of forgiveness is particularly pertinent to women living in relationships with immature men. You have forgiven him many times in the past but are painfully aware that nothing has changed. And you ask: How many times must I forgive him? How often can I be expected to overlook his hurtful remarks and destructive behaviour?

I am about to say something that may shock you, but I say it after years of studying the concept of forgiveness from theological and psychological perspectives. *You don't have to forgive if you don't want to.* Indeed, I will take it a step further and say: *It is wrong to forgive, it is spiritually and psychologically unhealthy to forgive, when forgiveness is not appropriate.*

My enquiry into the reasons behind the strong emphasis on forgiveness has led me to the following discoveries:

From justice to freedom

There has been a worldwide movement (at least in the Western world) away from a focus on justice and the need to do the right thing, to a focus on love and individual freedom. As the world became more and more dominated, in the 1980s, by economic theories, by big business concerns, by materialism, by individual and corporate greed, individuals were encouraged to look out for "number one". Today, they are often referred to as the "me" generation because the emphasis was on individual empowerment, ambition, competition, winning. Any talk of justice and fair play, any talk of living cooperatively with others, wouldn't have served the interests of those whose aim was to come out on top.

At personal and interpersonal levels, the emphasis was on love and freedom. It was a new era where everybody was supposed to be free to do their own thing. It seemed to make sense at the time but, looking back on it, what I see is that it was *men* who were free to do their own thing. Women were encouraged to love. Men were encouraged to take their freedom. While love is a strong emotion, the kind of love women were encouraged to have was weak. There was an expectation that women would be passive and accepting of their man's right to freedom. There was an expectation that she would be understanding and forgiving, no matter what he did. In that way, she would be "proving" her love for him.

The movement away from a focus on shared justice in relationships to a focus on freedom for men and love and forgiveness for women continues today. Some men, those who are mature, see the injustice and refuse to be a part of a system that is so unequal and unfair. Immature men, on the other hand, insist that they have a right to do their own thing regardless of the effect their behaviour has on others. Those who oppress others with their arrogant attitudes and immature behaviour are free to go on oppressing others, while the rest of us are supposed to be loving, accepting, understanding and forgiving. Very convenient!

The church has got it wrong

It is not uncommon to hear sermons in church about how important it is to forgive. Such sermons are often based on the conversation Christ had in which he was asked about how often we can be expected to forgive others. The answer he gave was "seventy times seven" which, we are told, means that there is no limit to the number of times we are to forgive a person who wrongs us. Let me say that a preacher who stops there is only giving us half the story and it is what is omitted that makes all the difference.

A more comprehensive study of the Bible reveals quite a different picture in relation to forgiveness. One thing it says is that you don't have to forgive people unless they are sorry for what they have done to you. Not only is it inappropriate to forgive someone who is not sorry but it is also *wrong*.* The correct response, when someone has hurt you, is to confront him and be angry with him. It is only when he says he is sorry that forgiveness is appropriate.

New Age and popular psychology has got it wrong

The church has got it wrong because it has allowed itself to be influenced more by the wishy-washy liberalism of New Age and popular psychology than by the demand for justice which exists in the teachings of Christ. Psychology has been very influential in our society and

---

* See Luke 17:3—"If your brother sins, rebuke him, and if he repents, forgive him."

popular psychology, in particular, exhorts us all to forgive. Don't focus on your hurts, they tell us. Just forgive everybody and be positive. This is the "don't worry—be happy" syndrome referred to earlier. New Age philosophy and teaching about forgiveness always sounds good but, frankly, it doesn't work. There is absolutely no point in *saying* you forgive someone who has wronged you if you don't feel it. There is a process which needs to be gone through if forgiveness is going to be real and effective. What is that process?

First, guilt must be acknowledged by both the guilty one and the victim. In simple terms, that means that the guilty one will say "I know I hurt you" and the victim will say "Yes, you did." When the guilt is confirmed in that way, the guilty one is then able to say "I'm really sorry for what I did to you." It is then that forgiveness becomes appropriate. To say that forgiveness becomes appropriate is not to say, however, that you must forgive. Just because your partner admits guilt and says he's sorry, it doesn't mean you have to forgive him immediately. Indeed, it doesn't mean you have to forgive him at all. It takes time to get over hurt and pain. For your own sake, you must take your time. If you force yourself to forgive before you are ready, it won't be real. And it is quite possible that you will *never* be ready to forgive a particular incident. You may feel that there are some crimes or sins which are unforgiveable no matter how sorry the perpetrator says he is. If that is the case, then any attempt to forgive would be inappropriate.

It is mainly women who are urged to forgive
In my study of forgiveness, this very interesting fact emerged. It is usually *women* who feel under pressure to forgive. This seems to parallel what we said earlier about

guilt (Situation 36). Just as women are ready to feel guilty about everything, even when they are not guilty, just as women apologise all the time for things they haven't done, so women feel the pressure to forgive almost before their partner has finished his insults or accusations or violence. It's as if women are saying: "It's all right. Hurt me again. I don't mind. I forgive you."

How is it that most women pressure themselves to forgive but men, generally, do not? There are several reasons, but I want to mention just three:

1. All the places the message of forgiveness is preached (the church, therapy, self-help books, women's magazines) are those accessed mainly by women.
2. Women are more open to suggestion than men, more willing to consider someone else's opinion, more ready to change and improve their behaviour.
3. Men are much more competitive, much more interested in winning. When someone hurts a man, his impulse is much more likely to be to get even, than to forgive.

This, of course, creates a seriously unbalanced situation in relationships. Women always ready to forgive, men determined to get even.

What needs to happen in order for relationships to be improved is, first, that those preaching false messages about forgiveness must stop. To urge (mainly) women to forgive in situations where forgiveness is inappropriate is to do untold damage to victim and perpetrator alike. Second, both women and men must give attention to the concept of forgiveness and try to develop a better understanding of it. And, finally, both women and men must be determined to observe the proper processes of acknowledging guilt and offering forgiveness if and when it seems appropriate to do so.

Suggestions for action

Only forgive when forgiveness is appropriate

To reiterate what was discussed above, when you have been hurt by your partner, it is appropriate to offer forgiveness, provided:

- you raise the issue with him and he is willing to discuss it
- he acknowledges your hurt
- he feels sorry
- he tells you he is sorry
- he takes definite steps to ensure he won't repeat the offending behaviour.

Of course, there is no way of knowing for certain if his remorse and apology are genuine but, until proved otherwise, it is a good idea to accept them as genuine. Once he goes through this process, then it is appropriate to forgive him. But, only offer forgiveness if you feel you can do it honestly.

Don't say you forgive when you don't feel it

Getting to the point of genuinely being able to forgive someone often takes time. Take your time. Don't be bullied or rushed into it by your partner's need to feel forgiven or by all those pressures coming at you from friends, family and society in general. Offer forgiveness only when you are ready, only when it feels right.

Let go of the anger and hurt

As already discussed, you may never get to a point where you feel you can forgive your partner for what he did. There are some behaviours which are really difficult to forgive. He may have sexually abused your child. He may have assaulted you. He may have had an affair. He may have left you without warning. If forgiveness isn't appropriate for you, then don't forgive him. Don't even try. But do try to get to a point where you can let it all go. It is very bad for you to hold on to hurt and pain and anger. Some people hold on to such feelings for years. Some never let go of them and are bitter and controlled by them till the day they die.

Whatever you do, don't let your partner's betrayal control you and turn you into the kind of person you don't want to be. Remember, you don't have to forgive but you do have to let it go. How can you do that? The best way is to find a counsellor or friend who will encourage you to release your emotions. Acknowledge that you have a lot of pain and sadness and anger inside you. Once you have expressed and worked through all those emotions, you will feel like a new person. Get them out. Get rid of them. And then you'll be able to make the most of your life.

38. When your self-esteem needs a boost

Self-esteem became an "in" word in the 1980s and continues to receive attention in self-help and popular psychology books to this day. I wholeheartedly agree with those who say that it's crucial to have a good self-esteem. Put simply, if you want to have a happy life, you must like yourself. That's the bottom line.

But lots of women don't like themselves. At least, that's what it sounds like when I hear how often they put themselves down. I used to do it, too, but not any more. I learned a long time ago that, every time I put myself down, I was inviting others to think of me in the same way. When I gave out messages that I didn't like myself, I was telling other people that I wasn't worth liking. Since I stopped doing that, people seem to like me a lot more. Evidence of low self-esteem can be found in the things a woman says about herself:

'I'm too fat'.

'I wish I didn't have such big hips'.

'I hate my hair'.

'I wish I was taller'.

'I can't stand looking in the mirror and seeing all my wrinkles'.

'I wonder why my husband stays with me'.

'There's no way I'm going to speak in a group and show my ignorance'.

'I don't know anything'.

'I'm not worth listening to'.

'My kids are smarter than I am'.

'I could never learn computers. I'm too dumb'.

And the list could go on and on. Sometimes it seems to me that women compete with each other to see who can say the worst things about herself. When a woman takes every opportunity to put herself down, she is revealing that she has very low self-esteem.

Other evidence can be found in what a woman does. She might:

- keep quiet in mixed company and let her husband do all the talking
- when asked a direct question, look to her partner to answer on her behalf
- walk with her shoulders slightly stooped
- avoid eye-contact with others, as if to say "Please don't notice me"
- develop a fear of going out and find every excuse to stay at home
- do nothing to improve her general knowledge (e.g., never read newspapers or listen to informative programs on radio or TV).

Again, the list could go on and on.

Sometimes, in counselling, women tell me that they can remember a time, during their teenage years or early twenties, when they had a really strong self-esteem. They were proud (even arrogant). They had an opinion about everything and weren't afraid to express it. They were rebellious and were mostly not affected by their parents' opinions or criticisms. Most of these women look back on that time as a time when they were happy. Yes, they may have done a few things they wish they hadn't done, but they remember really liking themselves and being happy with who they were.

What is it that happens to women? What happens to cause our self-esteem to sink lower and lower? It seems to have something to do with the way we relate to men. Lots of women have the idea that loving a man means they have to give themselves away to him and, consequently, once they get involved in a relationship, they focus almost exclusively on their partner and lose sight of themselves.

When we examine the development of self-esteem, we see that it is closely related to esteem by others. It is much easier to like yourself if you know other people like you. Alternatively, if someone puts you down, you are more likely to put yourself down. Any woman in a relationship with a partner who puts her down constantly will soon develop low self-esteem.

I have a sister who spent years feeling pretty bad about herself. Even though she had three lovely children during that time and was an exceptionally good mother, her self-esteem was never good. Why? Because her husband, the father of her children, was an immature man who had to put her down constantly so that he could feel like a big man. As soon as she found the courage to leave him, she started feeling better about herself. Then, she met a man who was mature and had no need to put others down. Instead of insults and ridicule, my sister began receiving affirmation and respect. Needless to say, her self-esteem rocketed.

It is important for all of us to remember that the way we feel about ourselves is definitely connected with the kind of feedback we get from others. It doesn't have to be *limited* by that, as I will discuss in the following suggestions for action, but it is certainly connected.

Suggestions for action

If your self-esteem is in a downward spiral, how can you give it a boost? How can you begin to feel good about yourself and develop a strong and healthy self-esteem?

Develop your self-knowledge

Know who you are. Make up your mind that you are not just going to drift along from day to day being whoever anyone else wants you to be. Be your own person. Before you can be your own person, of course, you have to know who that person is. There are several ways that you can go about developing a better awareness of who you are.

One way is to set aside some time, periodically, when you can be by yourself and ask yourself questions, like: Who am I really? Regardless of what my partner, or anyone else, says about me, what kind of person do I see myself to be? What makes me happy? What makes me unhappy? What makes me uptight? What makes me relaxed? What makes me angry? How well do I communicate? How well do I express my feelings? These are the kinds of questions you need to ponder. Women, generally, are quite good at being self-conscious, that is, conscious of themselves. In fact, sometimes we focus too much on ourselves and the focus is often negative. For example, after we've had a conversation with someone, or after we've spoken up in a group discussion, we can so easily go into destructive self-scrutiny. "Why did I say that? I bet they all thought I was stupid. If only I had kept quiet. I wonder if anyone noticed how uptight I was." And so on.

That is not the kind of self-questioning I'm recommending. That kind of negative criticism of yourself is too easy, and it doesn't achieve anything. When I suggest setting aside time to reflect on yourself, I want it to be a positive exercise. I want it to be a first step toward developing a healthier and more realistic awareness of your self.

Another way of developing a better awareness of yourself is to look at your life in all its facets and ask yourself how well you are doing in each facet. I suppose it could be called taking an inventory of yourself. What I am calling "facets" of our lives are: physical, emotional/psychological, intellectual, spiritual and social. You might like to get a piece of paper and make these areas into five headings and then proceed to address them one by one. If you start with "physical", ask yourself: What am I like physically? How well do I take care of my physical needs? Do I get enough exercise? Do I eat healthy foods? Do I feel healthy? Do I like the way I look? And so on. Then do the same thing with "emotional/psychological" and so on through all the areas. Taking such an inventory from time to time will keep you in touch with who you are and how you are progressing.

A third way of developing a better awareness of yourself is to look at your life over time. In other words, look at yourself as someone who has a past, a present and a future. Be aware that who you are in any *present* moment is affected by the hurts, the regrets, the happy experiences of your *past* as well as by your plans and aspirations for the *future*. When you decide to take an honest look at yourself in this way, be warned that it can be as distressing as it is rewarding. If you have painful memories from the past which you have, till now, pushed away and, if you decide it's time to dig them out and face them with a view to taking control of their effect on you, it might be a painful exercise. Maybe you should consider asking a counsellor to help you through the worst of it. Looking at yourself in terms of the time segments of your life (past, present, future) is a very helpful thing to do in your quest to develop a healthy self-awareness.

Look objectively at the feedback you get from others

Because negative feedback, or criticism, can erode our self-esteem, it is crucial that we not automatically accept all the criticism which is levelled at us. Remember that criticism from an immature man is usually his way of making himself feel superior. There is often no truth, or very little truth, in the accusations he makes. Also, criticism from one's children is often not reliable. Children, like immature men, can be pretty self-centred. They have their own agenda. And often their criticism of you has nothing to do with anything you may or may not be doing, and everything to do with making themselves feel big and powerful.

When criticism is levelled at you, try not to take it to heart. Develop the ability of pushing it a little distance away from your emotions so that you can consider it objectively.

Deliberately work to develop your confidence
and assertiveness

Just as a healthy and realistic self-awareness helps boost your self-esteem, so does confidence and assertiveness. Work at developing your self-confidence. Learn what it means to be assertive (see Situation 40), and have the courage to say and do the things you want to say and do. The more you see yourself being who you want to be, the better you will feel about yourself.

Gather people around you who like you and who will
give you positive feedback

If positive feedback about ourselves is what we need in order to improve our self-esteem, then we must shake off those who insist on putting us down. I know it's not possible, or even advisable, to shake off your dependent children when they are the source of constant criticism, but it is possible (and advisable) to shake off a partner, so-called friends, relatives and adult children who persist in criticising you to satisfy their own need to feel that they are better than you. You don't need those kinds of people in your life.

First, tell them you are tired of all the negative feedback and you want them to stop. Tell them you want them to start focusing on your positive attributes and giving you feedback about those instead. If they persist in their criticism of you, if they are intent on dragging you down and making you feel bad, flick them out of your life. It may take a while to replace them but, no matter how long it takes, make it your business to replace them with people who like you and want the best for you. Life is too short to waste it on those who are intent on putting their own problems on you. Gather around you people who think you're great, and your self-esteem will improve in leaps and bounds.

Jacky Fleming (1992). *Never Give Up*. London: Penguin.

39. When you are terrified of being alone

There are different kinds of loneliness. There's the loneliness you feel sometimes when you're surrounded with people and there's the loneliness you can feel when you are alone.

While you are not alone in the physical sense when you're surrounded with people you can, nevertheless, feel desperately lonely. I remember going to a conference for psychotherapists and counsellors a few years ago. It was a bit daunting going by myself to a conference in another city where I was pretty certain I would know nobody, but I'm a confident person, and I was sure it would be all right.

As we gathered for drinks and speeches of welcome on the first night, it didn't take me long to realise that almost everybody there knew each other—except me. As participants arrived, there were raucous greetings between friends who hadn't seen each other for a long time. No one greeted me. There were hugs and expressions of genuine affection all round. No one hugged me. Occasionally, there was a polite nod from someone who was walking past me to greet someone else. What does one do in those situations? I tried to take the initiative a couple of times by starting up conversations but, in each case, someone else came along and I was relegated to the position of observer as the other two chatted away happily. After a while, I took to moving around the room by myself observing the artwork which hung on the walls. To avoid the embarrassment of appearing to be a "shag on a rock", totally out of place, a misfit, I tried to give the impression (as if anyone cared!) that I was an avid connoisseur of art. What a disaster of an evening! I couldn't remember ever feeling so lonely.

Some women who attend cocktail parties or barbecues arranged by their husband's employers have a similar experience to mine and they come to dread those occasions with a passion. They tell me they try to get out of going but it is usually an unspoken expectation that employees will be accompanied by their partners. Such gatherings can be dead boring for the spouses and a source of loneliness, embarrassment and anxiety.

Another place where women can experience loneliness in a group of people is in their own homes. I mentioned earlier the fact that wives and mothers are expected to be available to support husbands and children all the time, but that nobody sees the need to support the women. If a man needs to talk about the awful day he has had, his partner tries to find the time to listen. But when it is her turn to talk about the dramas of her day, he is too tired to listen. He just wants to relax in front of the TV. Also, when a child comes home from school in tears, Mum is there to listen and smooth the jagged edges. But when she needs someone to help her or listen to her, the children are too busy doing their own thing.

In all the situations discussed above, there is a lot of loneliness for women. When all you want is a decent relationship but, instead, you have to put up with being the butt of jokes, being ignored, lied to, abused, betrayed, when you are deprived of attention and respect, it can be a very lonely road.

While the loneliness a woman feels in her relationship can be a terrible experience, most women seem to prefer that form of loneliness to the loneliness they imagine they would feel if they left the relationship. Most find the thought of actually being physically alone a terrifying thought. It is for that reason that most women are prepared to put up with extremely bad treatment at the hands of their partner. It is for that reason that women refuse to leave a destructive relationship unless and until they find another man. They are prepared to leave a bad relationship to move into a new one (which could end up being just as bad) but they are not prepared to leave their bad relationship to be by themselves.

It's puzzling. Why are so many of us so terrified of being alone? Is it because we think we can't manage financially and/or emotionally? Is it because we think the children will miss out on something if their father isn't there in the house? Is it because we don't like ourselves and dread the thought of being alone with ourselves? Is it because we need to feel that we belong to someone and that a bad husband is better than no husband?

As a therapist working with women and men, I have puzzled over this for many years. Why do so many women find a destructive relationship preferable to being alone? At the base of it all, I believe, is the way we are socialised as girls. While boys learn early on that men are not valued very highly if they don't have a job, girls learn that women are not valued very highly if they don't have a relationship. For most teenage girls and women, being in a relationship is a sign that they are making a success of their lives. Any other signs of success, such as getting a university degree, excelling in sport, getting a job, having a career, are nothing compared with having a relationship. It doesn't even have to be a successful or a good relationship, so long as you can be seen to be attached to a man. Romance novels, teenage magazines, women's magazines all play a part in this destructive kind of conditioning, with stories of girls and women being only too prepared to give up sporting careers or jobs or the desire to travel once they meet Mr Right. The expectation is that women will sacrifice everything for the sake of their relationship and that they will be happy doing it. The result of all this conditioning is that most women fear being alone, and "alone" means being without a partner.

If you recognise in yourself a fear of being alone, it is crucial that you work to change that. To fear something which may, in fact, occur due to circumstances over which you have no control, is to cause yourself to live with a terrible sense of vulnerability and powerlessness—the very stuff anxiety attacks and depression are made of. Life is such that any one of us could be left suddenly alone if our partner dies or chooses to separate from us. If our attitude toward being alone is one of fear and terror, the loss of a partner can mean the loss of emotional stability and the loss of hope for the future.

The first thing women need to do is to acknowledge that it is impossible to control everything in life, that we are, to some extent, subject to the circumstances which exist around us. Then, we need to give some thought to the difference between being alone and being lonely. Being alone does not have to mean being lonely. It is natural, of course, that there will be a certain amount of loneliness when one's partner dies or leaves the relationship, but it does not have to be the kind of loneliness that is accompanied by fear and terror and desperation.

What is the difference between being "alone" and "lonely"? Aloneness has a positive connotation while loneliness is most often seen to be negative. I want to suggest that when the circumstances of our lives cause us to be without a partner, it is possible for us to choose between feeling alone or feeling lonely. If you are a woman who is experiencing deep loneliness, remind yourself that it would be easier to bear if you could think of what you're going through as "aloneness".

When one considers the fact that we are born as unique, individual people and that, when our time comes to die, we go through the passage of death totally alone, it becomes clear that aloneness is an integral part of life. Just as we can be said to be social beings who need to be with other people, so we can be said to be individual people who need to come to terms with our aloneness and to welcome and enjoy opportunities to be alone. A person who gets the balance right between being alone and being with others is well on the way to being a healthy and mature individual. To reject aloneness as a terrifying possibility is to reject a major part of who we are.

If you are aware of a fear or a reluctance in you about being alone, it is advisable to begin working on it before you are actually in a situation where aloneness is thrust upon you. Start acknowledging that you are a unique individual and celebrate that fact. Remind yourself that, no matter how much you might want to merge with someone else so as never to feel lonely again, it is an impossibility. There will always be a deep part of yourself which nobody but yourself will ever be able to understand or identify with. In this sense, you are alone in the world, so you may as well decide to enjoy it. Look for times when you can be by yourself so that you can work at getting to know yourself better. Enjoy your own company and celebrate the unique person that you are.

Once you feel comfortable with aloneness, you will be better equipped to deal with situations where you are forced to be alone. You will feel lonely and sad during those times but you will, also, have the strength to change your loneliness into aloneness. When aloneness is thrust upon you, you will choose to embrace it as something that has to be, rather than reject it and be terrified by it.

Suggestions for action

The following suggestions are simply a reiteration of the points made above.

Understand the difference between being alone and being lonely

Being alone can be a positive thing, while sinking under the weight of fear and terror at the thought of being lonely, is negative.

Acknowledge that you are alone in the world and celebrate your aloneness

You are one-of-a-kind! A unique, individual person! This is a fact which ought to be celebrated, not feared.

Choose aloneness over loneliness

When circumstances force you to be alone, choose to interpret your situation, not as forced emptiness and loneliness but, rather, as an opportunity for aloneness, an opportunity for you to explore your own creativity and strengthen your connections with the wider community.

40. Finding the courage to live assertively

We only have one life, and this is it. My philosophy is that I had better live this life to the full because it's the only chance I'm going to get. I sometimes think about how terrible it must be for those people who get to the end of their lives and have to admit, when it's almost too late, that they wasted the only life they'll ever have.

Psychologist Erik Erikson wrote about this in the 1960s. He said people spend the last years of their lives with a sense either of despair or of integrity. Those who experience feelings of despair are those who are filled with regret as they look back over their "one and only life" and see wasted years, missed opportunities and unfulfilled dreams. In their depression and despair, they seem to be saying: "If only . . .". Those who experience feelings of integrity, on the other hand, are those who look back over their lives with a sense of satisfaction and achievement. The word "integrity" refers to the need we all have to feel that all the parts of our lives have been integrated (have come together). In old age, we can look back and feel good about the fact that it all came together for us. There were bad times, there were struggles, there were decisions to make, there were situations which caused us distress at the time but, still, we were able to make it all come together in a way that makes us now feel whole.

That's the way I want to spend the final years of my life. Wait! Let me correct that. What I meant to say was: That's the way I *intend* to spend the final years of my life. I have tested the boundaries of my life and broken through—and now it's up to me.

I don't mean to give the impression that all women have the power simply to *choose* the way they will live their lives because it isn't true. Some live in extreme poverty. Some live with a disability. Some live with a mental illness. Some live with the threat of extreme violence to themselves and their children and, whenever they have tried to leave their violent partners in the past, they were found, dragged back, and subjected to hideous and inhumane treatment. None of these women has freedom of choice. But there is a sense in which we can all confront our boundaries, at least in our minds, acknowledge the circumstances of our lives, and make decisions about how we will live. Some will, of necessity, make their decisions within the boundaries imposed upon them, while others will be able to burst through the boundaries.

In order to arrive at the end of our lives with a sense of integrity and well-being, we must find the courage to live assertively—now. It is how we live in the present moment, in *every* present moment, which determines the way we will be in old age. I recommend assertiveness. How can you live assertively? But, first, what is assertiveness?

The easiest way I have found to understand what it means to live assertively is to compare it with the idea of living passively or living aggressively:

- *Passive.* A passive person is one who allows others to walk all over her.* If you have the *choice* to allow or disallow someone's dominance and you give in to it, then you can be said to be acting passively. Some women, when dealing with their children, can be quite assertive (sometimes even aggressive). But, in

---

* A woman who gives in all the time to her violent partner is not necessarily being passive in her subservience. She could be assertively choosing survival for herself and her children.

relation to their partner, they are passive all the time. It's almost as though they have had life's spark crushed out of them by his immature, domineering attitudes and behaviour, and have given up. The only time they feel free to be themselves is with their children.

- *Aggressive.* In contrast to a passive person who lets others walk all over her, an aggressive person is one who walks all over others. Aggressive words and behaviour are usually very hurtful and destructive. Some women are aggressive a lot of the time, putting their partner down at every opportunity and being constantly critical of the children.

- *Passive-aggressive.* Many women are guilty of dominating others in a different way, that is, with their moods. Such behaviour is called passive-aggressive. Most women who behave in this way would reject the suggestion that they are being aggressive because, they would argue, they are not yelling or physically abusing anyone. The fact is that by using behaviour which seems to be passive, they effectively control the lives of everyone around them. By sulking, pouting, withdrawing, refusing to speak and generally causing gloom and fear to descend on the household, they are being very aggressive indeed.

None of the above behaviours (passive, aggressive or passive-aggressive) is recommended. They all leave you feeling frustrated and unhappy and have a very negative effect on relationships. I highly recommend that you learn how to live assertively and begin relating to your partner and children (and everyone else) in an assertive way. What does it mean to live assertively? It means you believe in your right to have your own opinions and to express those opinions, to have your opinions listened to, to say "no" and mean it, to insist that you are taken seriously, to tell people how you feel, to make requests of other people and to be treated with respect.

Many women have told me, over the years, that whenever they try to be assertive, their partner and others accuse them of being aggressive. Don't let that worry you. Anyone who has gained from your passivity in the past—that is, anyone who has been able to dominate you in the past because you have been so passive—is not going to like it when you begin acting assertively. To accuse you of being aggressive is their way of trying to get you to revert to your old ways. Don't be fooled. So long as you know the difference between assertive and aggressive, you can be confident that you are actually being assertive when you think you are. One example: when you say, firmly and angrily, "I'm really furious at you for the way you spoke to me last night in front of our friends", you are being assertive. But if you say, "You make me sick! You were nothing but a foul-mouthed, drunken slob last night when our friends were here", you're being aggressive. An assertive person doesn't resort to name-calling and put-downs but, rather, asserts her right to say how she feels and to say it as strongly and as passionately as she wants to.

Another example: when a man wants to have sex with his partner and she doesn't want it, a passive woman will either say nothing or look for excuses, the result of which is that she gives unclear messages. Then if her partner, thinking only of himself, goes ahead and has sex with her anyway she, martyr-like, puts up with it and feels terrible afterwards. An aggressive woman, in that same situation, will say something like: "After the way you treated me last week when our friends were here? You've got to be joking! I wouldn't have sex with you if you were the last man on earth!" An assertive woman, on the other hand, will simply say "no", and say it clearly and unambiguously. "No, I don't feel like it tonight. Let's just have a cuddle and go to sleep." She doesn't resort to making up excuses because she believes her "no" ought to be enough. She expects to be taken seriously and treated with the respect she deserves. If her partner persists, she persists right back. No matter how long he goes on about it, she continues to say "no" if she means "no".

To be assertive is to know what you want or don't want, and to have the courage to say so as clearly as possible without putting the other person down.

Suggestions for action

Don't waste your life being passive

Make up your mind that you aren't going to be one of those people who approach the end of their lives in despair. If you passively give your life over to someone else's domineering ways, if you find yourself always being the martyr, if you suppress your own desires and opinions in favour of those of your partner, you will arrive at the last stage of your life with the feeling of having been cheated. You will sense, at that late stage, that you gave your one and only life away to others and, through your despair, you'll say: "If only my life had been different."

If it is within your power to stop thinking and speaking and acting passively, do it now. Be determined that you are not going to waste your life, your dreams, your opportunities.

Test the boundaries of your life

If you are in a situation from which it is impossible to free yourself, at least test the boundaries. If you are a woman with a disability, don't be satisfied with the limits others place on you. Test the limits and be as assertive and as active as you can be within those limits. If you are a woman with a mental illness, don't be satisfied with the limits other people place on you. Many people who aren't familiar with mental illness will give you messages which say you ought to *act* like a person with a mental illness (whatever that means!). Certainly, be committed to taking your medication and keeping yourself as well as you can be, but test the boundaries and live your life assertively. If you are a woman who is in a violent relationship from which you cannot escape, give in to your partner only to the extent that you need to to ensure the safety of yourself and your children. Push at the boundaries as much as you dare and be assertive within the limits imposed on you.

If, on the other hand, you are one of those women who live within boundaries which are *self*-imposed, that is, boundaries which exist simply as a result of their own passivity or lack of courage, admit it to yourself right now. Make up your mind that you will begin to push at the boundaries. Don't be satisfied with a life that is less than it could be. Burst through the boundaries.

Learn about assertiveness

Seek out books on assertiveness. Most women have to unlearn our old passive behaviours and teach ourselves new assertive behaviours. If you hear of an assertiveness course being offered, or a course on how to develop self-confidence, have the courage to take it.

Live assertively

The first step in learning how to live assertively is to make up your mind (assertively) that you are going to change from passive or passive-aggressive to assertive.

You can actually take that first step right now. You can say: "Yes. I am going to learn how to be more assertive."

That decision, of course, must be followed up immediately by the next step which is: go to the library today (or tomorrow) and check out a book which teaches assertiveness. Then, read it and begin practising new ways of behaving. Practise on your partner, your children, your friends. The secret of success, in learning how to be assertive, lies in the practice. Practise a new behaviour over and over till you get it right.

Living passively drains away your energy. Living aggressively causes you to live with constant regrets about what you said and did. But living assertively fills you with energy and gives you a new zest for living.

41. Becoming strong, growing stronger

Sometimes women tell me they are afraid of becoming "too strong" and they give two reasons. One is that they don't ever want to appear to be stronger, or more intelligent, or more assertive, or more opinionated than their partners. They don't want to "hurt his ego" or intimidate him by appearing to be stronger than he is, in any way. They express concern that men are turned off by women who are smarter or stronger. The sad thing about that is that often a woman *is* smarter and emotionally stronger than the man she lives with and the men she works with, but she feels she has to pretend she isn't.

It is true that some men *are* turned off by a woman's strength, but they are the immature men. A man who is mature and confident in his own abilities is usually quite happy to relate to women as equals regardless of how strong or intelligent the women are.

The other reason women give for being reluctant to develop their own strength is that they are afraid they might turn into hard, uncaring, domineering women. But that never happens. When I talk about strength, I'm talking about inner strength which is projected outwards, not a show of strength aimed at dominating others. That kind of "strength" is actually weakness. To develop one's inner strength is to develop a calmness, a gentleness, an enhanced self-esteem, a confidence and an ability to speak up for oneself and others.

When I run self-development groups, I often ask participants to think of two adjectives to describe the kind of person they think they are or the kind of person they would like to be. Then I ask them to tell the rest of the group their two adjectives. When it comes to my turn, I usually say: "I am strong and gentle." These two attributes are so important to me. People who have the wrong idea about what it means to be strong would say that it's a contradiction to want to be strong and gentle at the same time. They see gentleness as passive, weak, self-effacing, self-denying. But, they're wrong. Gentleness (in women or in men) is one of the indicators of inner strength. If we can be with others, listen to others, speak with others, relate to others in an attitude of gentleness, we are exhibiting real strength. It doesn't mean you'll never get angry. It doesn't mean you'll never assert yourself. It means that you will do those things and do them well. Because you are strong!

I stated in the introduction that the purpose of this book was to help us all become more honest about what's happening in our relationships and about what effect our relationship with our partner is having on our lives. In relation to women, I said I wanted women who live with immature men to open their eyes and have the courage to see how their relationships were affecting them. I said I wanted this book to help women to "decide to stop using up so much energy trying to infuse maturity into a man who prefers to be immature; stop blaming themselves for a situation that is not their fault; gain a greater understanding of their own feelings of disappointment and emptiness and loneliness; and begin to look at their options for a better future" (p. 6).

Regardless of what you decide to do about your relationship, that is, whether you decide to leave or stay, your options for a better future begin with the issues dealt with in Situations 36 to 41. Refuse to take on guilt that isn't yours. Don't allow yourself to forgive when forgiveness isn't appropriate. Develop ways whereby you will enhance your self-esteem. Celebrate your uniqueness and enjoy opportunities for aloneness. Push at the boundaries of your life and live assertively. And, above all, never be afraid of your own woman-strength.

Be strong. Grow stronger. Live boldly.

Jacky Fleming (1992). *Never Give Up*. London: Penguin.

Afterword

As a psychotherapist, I was aware of all the books out there about relationships – written with women in mind – because women are the ones who worry about their relationships, who lie awake at night trying to figure out what *they* are doing wrong to cause their husbands or boyfriends to treat them with so much contempt, trying to find the key to open their partner up so that he'll finally start communicating.

Women whose relationships cause them distress, look for books about relationships all the time. And the strange thing is that they actually want to read that it is they who are to blame for the problems in their relationship because, if I am to blame, I can do something about it. If I'm to blame, I will gladly change my behaviour. There's hope. And that's what most books about relationships trade on: they exploit women's desperate need for hope, by giving them false hope.

I knew as a psychotherapist and a feminist that, so often, it's not the woman's fault when things go wrong. When a man refuses to communicate with his partner, when he shows no respect for her, when he chooses to be violent or demand sex all the time or spend all his spare time consuming pornography, there's absolutely nothing a woman can do. She can change her approach to him, she can be more understanding, she can be the perfect wife – but it won't change him one iota.

So, I wondered if I could write a book about relationships that was totally honest. Frankly, it would have been much easier to write *Men are from Mars, Women are from Venus*. Making light of the desperate situation so many women are living with day after day in their relationships with men would have been easy. Urging women to be more patient with men, to accept their bad behaviour without question because, really, men are from Mars and you shouldn't actually expect to understand them. Just make allowances for them! Just be there for your man, keep all your hurt inside and love him no matter what he does.

Now, I don't mean to imply that those kinds of books are all bad. When I was writing my book, I made it my business to read the ones that were most popular and I found that there were some helpful things in some of them. *Women Who Love Too Much*, for example, has some useful advice for women but, the bottom line still is, if you are having problems in your relationship, it's probably your fault because you love too much. The author, Robin Norwood, encourages a woman to see it as *her* problem, and her problem is one of "co-dependency". And what she needs to do is enter into Norwood's ten-step programme toward "recovery". But is this fair? When a man consistently behaves in unacceptable ways, it is the *woman* who needs to recover from *her* problem. Now, if I had written that book, the title would have been quite different. Instead of *Women Who Love Too Much*, I would have called it: *Men who love themselves so much that they don't give a damn about their partner*. And, of course, the content would have been very different too.

Then, there's the book *How to Live with a Difficult Man*, full of advice to women about what to do, when to do it and how to survive. If I had written that book, it would have been called, not *How to Live with a Difficult*

Man but *How to Leave a Difficult Man* or, simply, *Why bother?* It's crazy the way women are encouraged to turn themselves inside out, to expend enormous amounts of emotional energy, second-guessing, tippytoe-ing around difficult men. And blaming themselves when it all gets too hard.

Is it any wonder that women continue to suffer from depression and anxiety at alarming rates? You can't live in denial and get away with it. You can't take all the blame on yourself when you're not to blame and get away with it. Deluding yourself in that way has serious effects on your mental, and often physical, health.

And then there appeared the really destructive book by Laura Doyle, *The Surrendered Wife*. I think the word "surrender" is a very interesting one in the context of relationships. The very word "surrender" has connotations of war. An army which is totally dominated, outmanoeuvred, outgunned by the enemy often has no other option but to surrender. And when Laura Doyle suggests surrender as the only path to a "happy" relationship, the only conclusion one can draw is that the man, the partner, is in effect the enemy – and that his behaviour is dominating and aggressive.

When a woman finds herself in a relationship with a man who treats her badly, I believe she has three options. She can surrender, as Laura Doyle suggests; she can spend her life trying to accept the way he is, trying to figure out ways to get him to change, as most other authors suggest; or she can let him know that she expects him to grow up and begin behaving like an adult – as my book suggests.

Now, some people might worry about the fact that a *feminist* has written this book. If those people believe all the lies told about feminists – that we hate men, that we encourage women to leave their marriages, etc. – of course they would think, without having read my book, that

that's what it's all about. Well, it's not. I want women to be happy. And if a woman is happily ensconced in a relationship with a man who respects her, communicates with her, sees her as his equal, what more could a therapist like myself want? If she is in a relationship with a man who doesn't respect her, etc., then she must do something about that.

The one thing I absolutely refuse to do in my book is blame women for the problems men cause in relationships. And it seems to have worked. *HELP!* has been translated into twelve languages. People like it. I've lost count of the number of women who've contacted me since *HELP!* first appeared in bookshops thanking me for "knowing" what they go through and, then, writing about it. And when I actually showed the book to women who had come for relationship counselling and also, at the launch of the first edition – women would look at the Contents and say: That's me. Yes, that's me, too.

When you're always the one who's wrong. Yes.

Living with a bully. Yes.

When you have sex to keep the peace. Yes.

My book does speak to the experiences of many women. It may surprise you to know that men have contacted me too – to thank me. They tell me that they hadn't realised what they were doing to destroy their relationship, till they read my book.

One day I received a phone call from a woman who told me that she lives with her husband and two children in Adelaide. After months of relationship counselling which hadn't worked for them, her relationship with her husband was about to end. They were both sad that they hadn't been able to make it work. One day her husband picked up my book from his wife's bedside table and started reading it. When he finished it, he began talking with his wife – communicating, she said, in a way that he had never done before. Just recently, she phoned me again (three years later) to tell me that they're still together and, while there have been some ups and downs, the relationship is now solid. I love to hear such stories and to know that my book played a part in what surely is a mini-miracle. And the best thing for me is to know that people are responding to the book's honesty.

To the women who have read my book, let me say: Remember that a relationship is a two-way street and that the best relationships are those where there is mutual love and respect. Whatever you do, don't sell yourself short. Have an expectation that you will be treated well in your relationships – and insist on it. The outcome may surprise and delight you.

OTHER BOOKS FROM SPINIFEX PRESS

Beyond Psychoppression
Betty McLellan

In *Beyond Psychoppression*, Betty McLellan surveys the development of psychotherapy and exposes the inadequacies of Freudian psychoanalysis, humanistic therapies, sex therapy, new age and popular therapies. She challenges the myths about the reasons for women's mental and emotional illness.

ISBN 1-875559-33-7

Defiant Birth
Melinda Tankard Reist

Defiant Birth tells the stories of nineteen women from around the world who were told they should not have their babies because of perceived disabilities – either in the child or themselves. Facing silent disapproval and sometimes, open hostility, this book chronicles what happened when they went ahead and had their children anyway.

ISBN: 1-876756-59-4

ENOUGH
Patricia Hughes

In this powerful narrative, Patricia Hughes tells how she stayed in an abusive relationship, until finally she said: ENOUGH. This is an important and heartfelt personal guide for women in abusive relationships and for friends and family who want to understand and help. *ENOUGH* includes practical guidelines – seven identifiable steps to freedom from domestic violence – and a National Help, Support and Referral Guide.

ISBN: 1-876756-40-3

A Passion for Friends:
Toward a Philosophy of Female Affection
Janice G. Raymond

A Passion for Friends examines the ways in which women have created their own communities and destinies through friendship. It concludes with a focus on the contemporary women's movement and its networks and friendships – as well as the forces operating against friendship between women.

ISBN 1-876756-08-X

*If you would like to know more about Spinifex Press
write for a free catalogue or visit our website*

SPINIFEX PRESS
PO Box 212 North Melbourne
Victoria 3051 Australia
http://www.spinifexpress.com.au